O9-BUC-766

CHOICEMAKING
for co-dependents, adult children and spirituality seekers

Transitions Counseling Center
5432 Thunder Hill Road
Columbia, Maryland 21045

Sharon Wegscheider-Cruse

Health Communications, Inc.
Deerfield Beach, Florida

Sharon Wegscheider-Cruse
ONSITE Training and Consulting
Rapid City, South Dakota

Library of Congress Cataloging-in-Publication Data
Wegscheider-Cruse, Sharon, 1938 —
  Choice-making : for co-dependents, adult children, and spirituality
seekers.

  Bibliography: p.
  1. Alcoholics — Family relationships.
2. Co-Dependence.   3. Adult children of alcoholics.
I. Title.
HV5132.W44   1987   362.2'92   87-8716
ISBN 0-932194-26-5

© 1985   Sharon Wegscheider-Cruse
Reprinted 1987

ISBN 0-932194-26-5

All rights reserved. Printed in the United States of America. No part of
this publication may be reproduced, stored in a retrieval system or
transmitted in any form or by any means, electronic, mechanical,
photocopying, recording or otherwise without the written permission of
the publisher.

Published by Health Communications, Inc.
        Enterprise Center
        3201 SW 15th Street
        Deerfield Beach, FL 33442

Foreword

by
Joseph R. Cruse, M.D.
Founding Medical Director
Betty Ford Center for Drug & Alcohol Rehabilitation

Our imperfections have a symptom — pain. And pain signals dysfunction, injury, or some dis-ease that requires something to change before relief can occur. That something is frequently us. One of the more unexpected side-effects of change turns out to be growth!

But there are times when that pain is like a rock in our shoe — imperceptible, bearable, and unimportant, as compared to the immediate task at hand. Then after we remove it, its actual importance becomes clear. Now we see the deep impression it has made, and almost immediately we feel the relief and freedom and regained agility when we remove the rock. We look at our wounds and blisters in disbelief that we could have denied their seriousness, or even their presence, and certainly their influence for so long.

But no matter the number of rocks that find their way into our shoes, the human spirit, once enlightened, continues to look up and hope and learn and delight in each lesson. The human spirit continues to choose and change — and continues to remove rocks, one by one.

The "rock-in-the-shoe" syndrome serves Sharon as both adversary and laboratory in her unrelenting drive to interpret for us her concepts of rights, fairness, and the human potential for healing and growth. Her curiosity provides the energy and assertiveness to design, experiment, and research basic questions such as "Why God and His subjects so often seem at odds with one another!"

On occasion, she discerns a plan — and she shares those plans with us — plans in which CHOICES are recognizable and need to be made. We learn that our stores of present and future choices are great. She shows us how to be grateful for our former self, as we grow and transform beyond that person. These directions lead to a full excitement with our own spiritual molding as our inner beauty comes closer and closer to the surface.

And the process continues . . . and continues . . . continues . . . toward a form of Grace as we realize the permanency of CHANGE, through CHOICE!

Foreword

by Claudia Black, Ph.D., M.S.W.
President of ACT (Alcoholism, Children, Therapy)

Having been academically trained to be a psychotherapist, it was only upon entering the chemical dependency field that I heard and understood the concept of "recovery." Therapists most commonly assist clients to better understand themselves, to like themselves, to become more effective communicators. For some clients, we are more problem solving oriented, in which the therapy is often limited to weeks. For other clients, our work may extend to several months, and possibly years. Much of the time we are effective in assisting our clients, and are able to assist in affecting changes in how they live their lives. But many will need to return for more problem solving, to have someone listen, to find hope and meaning in their lives. What is often missing is a plan for recovery. Recovery is a process; it does not have an ending. One grows, matures, and continues along a continuum of growth. On a daily basis, one lives the process that entails recovery. CHOICEMAKING guides us through the recovery process.

Prior to 1980s, in the chemical dependency field, the term "recovery" was typically applied to the chemically dependent person. Treatment programs acknowledged the need for family involvement, but typically only offered services for adult family members — spouses, lovers, or parents. Most commonly, those services were limited to alcoholism education, and did not cover treatment of co-dependency. There were a handful of programs that offered an educational program for children. The concept of Adult Children was only beginning to emerge, and by the 1970s the concept was there, but not the education, nor the treatment.

Education, problem solving, assertiveness training is not adequate treatment for the family member in a chemically dependent family. They will not be able to make the appropriate changes that will allow them to heal and find a comfort within themselves. They will need a new set of rules, new guidelines. They need to be led through a process. They need hope that is not based on the chemically dependent person's behavior, but based on who they find themselves to be — their identity, their new-found abilities.

CHOICEMAKING is about recovery for the co-dependent, as well as the dependent person. Choicemaking not only addresses the dependent spouse, lover and parent, but also includes children of all ages. Sharon also helps the reader to understand co-dependency as it can affect a helping professional. Co-dependency is a treatable condition, and CHOICEMAKING describes how recovery is possible.

I believe, as Sharon does, that we exist to live and grow. We are alive, vital. In CHOICEMAKING, the final (or fourth) step in recovery is that we must Surrender to Choice. The description of what surrender means is invaluable. A "power greater than ourselves" is an essential part of being able to surrender to choice. CHOICEMAKING offers the reader the understanding that they will work with the Higher Power. With the premise that we are all co-creators in shaping our destinies, as creators we have an active role in our recovery.

Sharon Wegscheider-Cruse is a trailblazer in her presentation of issues that are known as co-dependency; she encapsulates those issues in a manner that delineates specific treatment for co-dependency. She is a pioneer in extending the treatment concept to include ongoing recovery. There are many bright, creative people, but only a small number who affect change. Sharon is honored with what I believe to be a positive self-fulfilling prophecy related to the guidelines of personal rights she outlines in CHOICEMAKING. She knows (1) her right to dignity and respect; (2) her right to set her own priorities; (3) her right to stand up for herself, and (4) her right and obligation to show her feelings. Once again, we are blessed to have another 'work' by Sharon.

Preface

The establishment of co-dependency as an illness has been a difficult task — a task that continues to require the efforts of professionals and co-dependents alike. This book is my contribution to establishing the illness of co-dependency as a reality — not merely as an interesting concept.

As founding Chairperson of the National Association for Children of Alcoholics (NACoA), I have been acutely aware of a need to share my thoughts about this important group of people. In friendship and peership with the board members of NACoA, I grew to be an even stronger Choicemaker. This group continues to be a source of great teaching and support for me.

I have good memories about the events leading up to the organization of NACoA, and I go into those events in Chapter 3. But I also have memories of the times I felt tongue-tied, confused and unsure if I could communicate even a fragment of what I knew inside about the family disease. I've gained clarity from the ideas, opinions and insights freely exchanged with my peers and friends.

My great hope and desire is that treatment programs find the way to include full co-dependency and adult child treatment in their programming. Full treatment of this kind may end up being a major influence in the intervention of the progression of both co-dependency and alcoholism.

Another important part of this book was sharing my own story. I am grateful to my family, my children, my mate, special friends — and especially to my Higher Power — for leading, pushing, loving, caring, and teaching me to trust. I made it and I learned that no one makes it alone. After years of "perceived aloneness," I've come home to my own relationships. Homecoming feels good, and vulnerability is worth it.

May you, the reader, take this journey through my book with me. My wish is that you finish the book with a greater sense of your being able to make choices for yourself in the direction of your own fulfillment.

Happy **Choicemaking** . . .

Prologue: A Personal Word

In my earlier book, *Another Chance*, I felt that it was important to share some of my personal journey. As an adult child who had grown up in an alcoholic home — and yet, a loving and caring home — I struggled to untangle the confusion, hurt, loneliness, fear and guilt that didn't fit with the love, attention and care that I felt from my parents.

In the process of disentangling and sorting out the inconsistencies and mixed emotions, I learned an important lesson: I was not alone. I found that there were thousands of others who felt a kindred confusion, similar experiences, similar struggles and tangled emotions. Over the past few years, I have received letters, telephone calls, and personal visits from many of you who shared my experience.

Since the writing of *Another Chance*, I have undergone many changes, and I have gone into detail about many of these changes in Chapter 3 — "My Story."

I have found that **Freedom From** a painful condition and making choices to change my life were both challenges. They were challenges, yes, but only the first steps in my own recovery process.

I had to take risks. And at times I had to grapple with fear and uncertainty. For me, as for many others, recovery has been a long, arduous, and sometimes painful process.

Yet the time came when I felt my life had become more manageable, and I learned to make choices.

Paradoxically, however, making choices and taking risks did not get easier in recovery. Sometimes I was so surrounded by good people and positive experiences that I often felt overwhelmed and unsure of my decisions. I felt as if I had regressed, slipped back into old pressures and routines.

Coming to face the many options in my life, and continually learning to simplify my life posed my purest challenge. Simplify, simplify! And, in the process, I sometimes had to leave behind good people and positive experiences.

There comes a time when we know we can't go back, can't return to a former way of life, no matter how inviting it seems. And yet we don't know what's next. Like a pilot, flying by the seat of his pants in a heavy fog, we don't know where we're going.

Even more disconcerting, we don't have the slightest notion of what we're supposed to be doing. This leaves us in a void, a blank, an emptiness. But it's just possible that in this void we come to terms with who we are, we discover our origins. And somehow, through the void, through the emptiness, there's a sudden spark of understanding, and we recognize our Higher Power.

I see these times of emptiness as times of transformation. And transformation does not happen just once — it doesn't take place at 8:00 p.m. on a Thursday night in February, like a two-hour TV special. Transformation is a process and each day is an occasion for transformation.

The notion of transformation has played a key role in my thinking about "Freedom To," and I agree with Anthony Padavano's definition in his book, *Belief in Human Life:*

> There is a great deal of difference between loss, change, and transformation. A loss is a step backward; a change is an opportunity; transformation is a step forward. The common denominator in these three realities is the fact that one must give up something. It is possible for both loss and change to lead to transformation, but it is not possible for transformation to occur unless something is lost and something is changed.

The quest for **personal freedom** has occupied men and women over the ages. What are some meanings of freedom?

Liberation from restraint
Choice and action
Boldness of conception and performance
Possession of privileges
Self-determination
Spiritual self-fulfillment.

A synonym for freedom is "independence." Independence is freedom from dependence — an essential stage of recovery. **Freedom To** our own fulfillment is another stage of recovery.

Here are some definitions of dependence:
That which is suspended
State of being attached to something else as its consequence
Relying on something else for support.

There are many kinds of dependence. Here are some of the kinds of dependence I'll be mentioning in this book — dependence on:

Alcohol	Mood/Mind-altering drugs
Power	Sex
Money	Work
Children	Parents
Loved one	Food

Perhaps one of the most subtle and insidious of all dependencies is the dependence on a **person** who is addicted to any of the items listed above.

Where there is a fixed, compelling focus on any situation in a relationship, that situation tends to pull the person away from other relationships. People surrounding the rigidly focused person (food addict, alcoholic, workaholic), become preoccupied with trying to get into the addict's life in a meaningful way. In many respects, the frantic and unremitting efforts to reach the addict become as compulsive as the behavior of the lost person. We refer to this state as **co-dependency.**

The prefix "co-" means "together, jointly or in conjunction." In this book, I will use "co-dependency" to describe a condition of chronic dependency, a state that keeps us from self-fulfillment and personal freedom. Persons afflicted with this condition will be referred to as "co-dependents."

This book is written in three main sections: **Freedom From, Freedom To,** and the final quest, **Spiritual Transformation.**

May you enjoy the journey, and may it provide you with a useful framework for some of the happenings (serendipity or grace) in your life.

Since I wrote *Another Chance*, my mother completed treatment for prescription pill and alcohol addiction. It was my pleasure and honor to receive treatment with her so I could better understand my relationship to her and my own behavior as an adult child. It was a time of beautiful healing. I was able to tell her how much I loved and appreciated her.

I have also known the fulfillment and satisfaction of seeing each of my three children reach their adulthood with hard work, integrity, care for others and a sense of self-worth.

Especially meaningful for me, I have married a mate who allows me to fulfill myself in whatever way feels right for me, and invites me to share his journey as well. We are able to share a spiritual venture together.

My husband, Joe Cruse, introduced me to an anonymous prayer that I would like to share with you:

TODAY

I asked God for strength that I might achieve.
I was made weak that I might humbly learn to obey.

I asked for health that I might do greater things.
I was given infirmity that I might do better things.

I asked for riches that I might be happy.
I was given poverty that I might be wise.

I asked for power that I might have the praise of men.
I was given weakness that I might feel the need of
  God.

I asked for all things that I might enjoy life.
I was given life that I might enjoy all things.

I asked for vision that I might control my future.
I was given awareness that I be grateful for the now.

I got nothing I asked for — but everything I had
  hoped for.
Almost despite myself, my unspoken prayers were
  answered.

I am among all people most richly blessed.

Recently, a very dear friend and holy man, Sam Hardy, told a small group:

"The trouble so many of us face is not the fact that we haven't been loved, but rather that we have not learned TO love."

Learning to love involves transformation, the result of making choices. Non-transformed persons pay a terrible price for the illusion of safety, the illusion of invulnerability. The transformed person becomes free.

My life the past few years has been full of discernment and discovery. It has been necessary to make choices and decisions in regard to people, work and lifestyle. Some of these choices have been hard for others to understand, and at times I, too, have felt doubtful and in question.

Yet the inner peace that I have felt and the path that seems to be put right in front of me to follow are personal signs for me that my life, like yours and everyone's, has a special meaning.

And as we go our separate journeys, let us go transformed and transforming, *Choicemakers* and spiritual seekers at home in the universe.

Acknowledgments

My special thanks to the many people who have helped me put together these ideas by allowing me into the privacy of their inner lives. The reconstruction/restoration community has been a rich source of information, research, inspiration and loving support. I owe more than words can say to the participants in these workshops and seminars, and I am especially indebted to the "stars" and to my dedicated group leaders.

My husband, Dr. Joseph R. Cruse, has been a continuous source of encouragment. He helped me refine my ideas and expand my vision. Joe supported my choice to fulfill a need I had to put these thoughts on paper. He took me to the Colorado mountains, where I wrote most of this manuscript. And he patiently kept me company through many late nights and long days of writing and rewriting, rewording and copying. His love and care for me made this book possible.

My special thanks to Mark Worden for challenging me, teaching me, and guiding me through this work. His warmth, genuine concern for both the reader and myself gently led me to a greater sensitivity in my writing skills. It was an honor to work with him.

My thanks also to the whole team at *The U.S. Journal* — especially to Gary Seidler and Peter Vegso. They have done a praiseworthy job in bringing co-dependency and adult child issues to the public through the written word. I am proud to be part of that team.

Dedicated To

Joseph, my husband
Patrick, my son
Sandra, my daughter
Deborah, my daughter
Anne, my mother

Contents

1

Varieties of Co-Dependency

Co-Dependency: Toward A Working Definition

Until recently, "co-dependency" was virtually unknown. Those who worked with alcoholics and others affected by chemical dependency focused primarily on the addicted individual. But counselors and other clinicians often felt that chemical dependency touched the whole family — that, in effect, spouses and children and relatives of alcoholics could become "co-dependents" — in a sense, addicted to the dysfunctional alcoholic family system.

It is significant that the term "co-dependency" does not appear in the *Dictionary of Words About Alcohol* — a reference that devotes seven and one-half pages in exquisite detail about the nuances of "alcoholism." But, after all, alcoholism, as a field of study, has been around much longer than family systems and co-dependency.

In the past few years, there have been numerous attempts to define co-dependency, to describe the phenomenon so that others in the field can become alert to co-dependency, and acquire knowledge and tools to help the co-dependents as well as the alcoholic.

Sondra Smalley, Director of Dependencies Institute of Minnesota, sees co-dependency as:

> . . . a term used to describe an exaggerated dependent pattern of learned behaviors, beliefs and feelings that make life painful. It is a dependence on people and things outside the self, along with neglect of the self to the point of having little self-identity.

Robert Subby, director of Family Systems, Inc., Minneapolis, describes co-dependency as:

> . . . an emotional, psychological, and behavioral condition that develops as a result of an individual's prolonged exposure to, and practice of, a set of oppressive rules — rules which prevent the open expression of feeling, as well as the direct discussion of personal and interpersonal problems.

I have devoted the last ten years of my life to exploring the realm of co-dependency, and my investigations have led me to develop my own definition of co-dependency.

CO-DEPENDENCY IS . . .

> . . . a specific condition that is characterized by preoccupation and extreme dependence (emotionally, socially, and sometimes physically), on a person or object. Eventually, this dependence on another person becomes a pathological condition that affects the co-dependent in all other relationships.

A Primer of Co-Dependency

Co-dependency is a lifestyle, a patterned way of relating to others. It's a way of interpreting experience. And it's a lifestyle with low self-esteem at the core.

Co-dependents suffer from a progressive focusing of attention on a target and a concomitant neglect of one's own feelings and needs.

The co-dependent person leads a life characterized by:

- An inability to have spontaneous fun, an inability to let go. ("Life is serious, not a game, and spontaneity cannot be trusted, because it means I'm not in full control.")
- Problems with intimacy. ("Don't trust . . . **anyone**, for that way lies betrayal and disappointment and pain.")
- Inability to know what normal behavior is. ("The way I feel . . . I wonder if I'm crazy?")
- An exaggerated need for the approval of others. ("I must always be on guard to keep from offending others. I must please them, always please them. Then they'll like me.")
- Confusion about making decisions. ("I can't decide — it's too complicated, I might make a wrong decision and it would destroy me!")
- Anxiety about making changes. ("I don't think I could handle it if I got that promotion.")
- Black and white judgments. ("I don't see any room for compromise. There are no shades of gray in this matter!")
- Fear and denial of anger. ("Anger makes me feel like I might explode, and it frightens me because I don't know what I might do — but I get angry anyway.")
- Lies and exaggeration, when it would be easy to tell the truth. ("I never lie. There's nothing wrong. I'm not angry.")
- Fear of abandonment. ("I'm no clinging vine, but I couldn't live without you!")

- Tendency to look for people to take care of. ("It's wonderful to be needed by others.")
- Need to control self and others. ("I can't let my guard down — life's a serious business." Or: "I'll show him — I just won't talk to him anymore!")

More than anything, the co-dependent person gets stuck in and feels powerless in one or more relationships or situations. The child feels trapped in her alcoholic family, trapped and alone, for there's no one to turn to, no one to confide in. The co-dependent husband feels powerless to do anything about his alcoholic wife.

And this sense of vulnerability, this sense of being engulfed and overwhelmed, carries with it chronic and often intense emotional pain. There seems to be no way out — no escape, no respite. The co-dependent cannot sever the ties. The co-dependent person seems almost **dependent** on the family alcoholic, as if there's a strong need to remain emotionally and physically attached.

Co-dependency often has its beginnings in one's relationship with an alcoholic parent or other family member, but co-dependency can become a generalized way of relating with others in the world.

Who is most likely to be affected by co-dependency?

- Spouses of alcoholics and spouses of other drug-dependent persons.
- Young children with alcoholic parents, grandparents, or siblings.

In short, the co-dependent is likely to be someone who lives in an intimate relationship with an addicted person. And co-dependency intensifies with proximity and frequency of contact.

But others can also become co-dependents. Recovering alcoholics themselves may discover during their recovery that they were in a co-dependent relationship with alcoholic or drug dependent parents, spouses, children or siblings.

The bizarre rules and distorted communications in dysfunctional, or troubled, family systems may stunt or impede normal emotional and behavioral development. Anyone who lives in a family of denial, compulsive behavior, and emotional repression is vulnerable to co-dependency — even if there is no alcoholism or chemical dependency in the family.

Finally, it is extremely important to recognize that professionals who work with addictive persons can themselves become co-dependents, developing "helping" relationships with alcoholics and other addicted persons. In effect, co-dependent therapists and counselors become accomplices — would-be helpers whose actions undermine and thwart therapeutic progress.

Some Common Co-Dependent Patterns

• A co-dependent spouse, Sandy, worried all day long about what her husband, Rick, was doing at work (preoccupation). And after work, Sandy wondered: Would Rick stop off for a drink on the way home? Maybe even three or four drinks? And he probably wouldn't be able to go to the meeting they had both planned on (projection). Sandy was hurt and angry **before** Rick even came home. While making dinner, she sampled most of the meal and hated herself by dinnertime (compulsive eating). Then he arrived. Sandy was feeling so hurt and angry by the time Rick came home, she didn't even speak to him. An hour after he got home they were in an argument. Sandy discounted her own thoughts, feelings and plans, as she centered herself around responding to Rick.

• Nancy's physician thinks that Nancy should probably cut down on drinking — she's shown for appointments with alcohol on her breath. And he thinks there's some potential problems in all the pills she's taking. But when he questions her about her drinking, she tells her doctor that she hardly drinks at all anymore. He's satisfied with her answer, and doesn't ask her any more questions about her drinking. but when he tells her that he's going to cut down on her prescriptions for Valium and Dalmane, Nancy gets very defensive and tells him that she'll find a new physician who will be more sympathetic to her nervousness and her insomnia. The physician relents and continues to see Nancy and fill her needs and prescriptions, and Nancy continues to drink and take pills.

• David is a psychologist who grew up in an alcoholic family. He knows the pain and rejection one feels when not given due attention. David has never resolved his own feelings of rejection. Healing has not taken place. Therefore, when one of David's clients **sounds** rejected or hurt, he stops whatever he is doing and makes himself available to his client. He often minimizes his own needs in an attempt to be everready for his clients.

What family dynamics, other than alcoholism, contribute to co-dependency? **The family secret. Family traumas. Family rigidity and dogma.** All these characteristics of families can set the stage for co-dependency.

Families with a secret, for example, become protective and guard the secret closely. They do not talk about it. They erect elaborate excuses and indulge in "Let's Pretend." Let's pretend Grandma's not dying of cancer. Let's pretend Gerri didn't commit suicide because she was involved in drugs. Let's pretend that Daddy really works late and doesn't have a girl friend.

Families who have experienced trauma contribute to co-dependency in ways similar to families with a secret: The traumatic issue — a handicapped child, the death of a parent — is never discussed openly. Rather than deal with the family trauma directly, rather than face the pain, family members avoid and suppress it. The handicapped child is coddled and over-protected to the extent that it never receives the kind of education and care that would allow it to achieve its potential.

Rigid families, families who carry an overload of traditional dogma about the roles of family members, also provide a prime breeding ground for co-dependency. What are the dogmas? Women can't (and shouldn't) earn their own living. Men should always be strong, and should take the full responsibility for providing a livelihood for the family members. Women are fragile and need to be protected. But, at the same time, they should always — ALL WAYS — be attentive, and even preoccupied, with the needs of others.

Co-dependency flourishes in families that teach "learned helplessness." Examples of learned helplessness are:

- The mother who takes all the responsibilities for her children, never allowing them to develop their own sense of autonomy and responsibility.
- The father who steps in and fixes his son's bike because he can do it faster, better.
- The husband who takes care of all financial matters because his wife doesn't/can't learn about financial matters.
- The parents who supply more than adequate money and support rather than allow their college-age child to cope with the slightest hardship.

Families who promote learned helplessness in their kids and who rely on manipulation and control of others through intimidation, sarcasm, finances, etc. — all follow the same fundamental dynamics:

In any family system that controls behavior through reward systems and emotional repression, there is a dynamic of fear and manipulation set up. In a system of fear and manipulation, there is a pronounced craving for the approval of others. The person **needs** or **becomes dependent** on the approval of others, in order to feel acceptable. The end result is a reliance on others, a need for external validation, rather than the kind of validation that comes from within, from a secure sense of self.

Let's take a closer look at some of the symptoms of co-dependency.

Denial or Self-Delusion

The denial and self-delusion of the co-dependent involves a complex intermingling of love, fear, hate, guilt — ultimately leading to a kind of emotional paralysis. The co-dependent feels powerless to change her life, powerless to make important decisions.

Recognition of the "sick relationship" — admitting that there's something horribly awry — would mean that the co-dependent would have to recognize her own role, her own dependency, her own dysfunctional behavior.

The co-dependent vigorously resists this kind of self-knowledge. Instead, the usual reaction is to "normalize the sick behavior." The co-dependent says, "Living with Ralph isn't as bad as it used to be."

Or the co-dependent contends, "Look, Mary has a few faults — we all do, don't we. So she drinks a little too much at times. What the hell, she's had a tough life. Besides, she's not **that** bad."

And Sonia, the co-dependent child, defends her dad. "Dad doesn't drink all that much any more. He really isn't as bad as he was when he was drinking a fifth a day."

Are these flagrant lies? Or a peculiar kind of selective blindness — an inability to perceive the destructive wavelengths emanating from the addict. Certainly one thing is true: The minimizing and rationalizing of the co-dependent is often deeply ingrained and truly believed — ingrained and believed in much the same way as the minimizing and rationalizing of the addicted person.

Dependency is, after all, a compulsive response to something that has special meaning — alcohol, drugs, money, food. In the case of co-dependency, one's attachment to another person gives meaning to life. Approval from a specific individual gives comfort, safety and self-worth to the co-dependent person.

And the result? The co-dependent protects the person in

his life who gives it meaning, denies that the relationship is troubled, denies addiction — both the addiction of the person to whom he is attached, and his own addiction, his own compulsive attachment . . . her co-dependency.

Compulsive Behavior

Stress. Low self-worth. Need for approval. Feelings of rejection and guilt.

What to do? Do something — anything — that will relieve stress, that will get approval and numb feelings of guilt and rejection. Accumulate external signs of approval. Pile up signs of worth.

Some co-dependents become driven in accomplishment, in achievement. This drivenness might be reflected in job performance leading to advancement; or in some form of public visibility and celebrity based on achievement; or in pursuit of money or advanced degrees.

The high-achiever presses on, no matter what — often to the detriment of personal health, happiness and quality of relationships. Accomplishment and performance are what count. Accomplishment and performance give the co-dependent a sense of worth that cannot be readily found elsewhere.

Other co-dependents display compulsive behavior by running through cycles of abdication and repetition. When the going gets tough, they simply abdicate. They find relief in dropping out of stressful relationships and high-pressure jobs. They pull away from people, events and areas in which they are co-dependent in order to escape the pressure.

They run. They don't stick around to work through the issues. Seeking geographic cures, they make escapes — but the only thing that changes is the scenery.

Will an alternate lifestyle be less stressful? Not for the co-dependent, because for the co-dependent the issues and conflicts have not been resolved, and they tend to repeat — they tend to find themselves in situations and relationships similar to the ones they fled.

Finally, there is the person who compulsively lives to satisfy the expectations of others. The people-pleaser moves cannily through life, always trying to figure out what others want. That's the key to approval and gratification: Figure out what others want. And then give it to them.

The people-pleaser develops sophisticated skills and becomes adept at manipulation and control. Yet the bitter paradox is that the people-pleaser ends up in a self-destructive trap, controlled and manipulated.

Frozen Feelings

The co-dependent person harbors deep emotional pain and a deep-felt sense of guilt. No matter how hard the co-dependent tries to manipulate and seek approval, the yearned-for approval never really comes. And guilt builds up as the co-dependent, fully aware, continues to engage in self-deceit and in dishonesty toward others.

Consequently, the co-dependent feels as though no one really understands, no one comprehends the loneliness, fear and isolation experienced by the co-dependent. The sense of isolation — real and imagined — engenders a sense of uniqueness.

Repeatedly hurt and rejected, the co-dependent has learned to keep sensitive feelings inside. And the feeling of uniqueness keeps her cut off from sources of potential support. The result? Loneliness increases, intensifies.

And with loneliness and isolation comes fear. And anxiety. And dread. Why dread? Why fear and anxiety? Because the co-dependent has a miniscule sense of self-worth and feels totally powerless. Yet the co-dependent compulsively tries to get a handle on as many situations as possible — tries, against all odds, to become a controller.

Feeling the need to take charge, and at the same time feeling powerless, means that the co-dependent must live with a great deal of ambiguity, uncertainty and fear.

There is the fear of being found out — the fear that one's true self will be revealed and it will be judged unworthy. There is the fear of relaxing, a fear that the entire structure of one's existence might fall apart, collapse like a shanty in a windstorm.

Fear and trepidation permeate the co-dependent's whole existence — fears of abandonment, loneliness and rejection. And above all, the dread of discount and annihilation.

Anger — The Frozen Fire Within

The co-dependent's efforts to control people and circumstances do not pay off. And as attempts to control increase, people seem to become less controllable, and the co-dependent feels frustrated, irritated, angry.

But not actively angry. Not "really" angry. The anger is suppressed, frozen, hidden behind the mask of a tight smile.

Red-faced and seething with rage, the co-dependent person smiles a frozen smile and insists, "I'm not angry. Not really."

The denial of anger, the self-deceit and dishonesty, feed into depression. As time passes, the mind becomes a warehouse of pent-up memories and hidden resentments. Hurt feelings and unresolved conflicts get crammed into the warehouse for days, weeks, and even years.

The many resentments and angry hurt feelings may seem to disappear. Eventually, however, the chronic stress of unresolved emotional hurts becomes manifest in serious health problems — ulcers, hypertension, heart disease, cancer. One's energy and vitality diminish. One's career can suffer. Marriages go on the rocks.

Here are a few signs of repressed rage that most of us can readily identify:

- A hair-trigger temper that explodes over trifles.
- Frequent feelings of disappointment in others, and a feeling of being let down.
- Avoiding relatives and friends.
- Rapid weight gains, losses, fluctuations.
- Chronic aches and pains — headaches, backaches, stomach aches or other idiopathic, intractable pain.

Even more troubling: Hidden resentments invariably dampen and numb other emotions — the positive emotions of joy and love. Engaged in an internal struggle to fight back painful feelings, the co-dependent person cannot show affection for loved ones.

Intimacy entails exposure and risk. It entails openness and the relinquishment of control. In order to stay in complete control, the co-dependent fends off intimacy. It's safer to be alone, safer to be isolated, safer to stay emotionally numb, frozen. The co-dependent feels like the person in the song by Paul Simon: "I am a rock, I am an island . . . a rock feels no pain . . . an island never cries."

Frozen feelings of anger lead to confused and inauthentic human interactions — just the opposite of what the co-dependent thinks will happen. Frozen anger doesn't protect. It doesn't make life run more smoothly.

Instead, relationships become more difficult to handle. They reach an impasse or fall apart altogether. Smoldering anger paradoxically destroys the very things the co-dependent hopes it will protect.

Hidden aggression may be so firmly imbedded that it's unconscious, automatic. If confronted, the "hidden aggressor" would vehemently deny such feelings. In fact, hidden aggression sometimes comes disguised as love and care.

Let's look at the varieties of behavior cloaking hidden aggression.

Collusion

. . . The father who gives money and support to an able-bodied 26-year-old son, seductively keeps his son in a state of dependency and prevents the development of self-reliance by meeting all the son's needs.

. . . The boss who gives candy and rich delicacies to an overweight secretary enters into a collusion with the secretary to pretend that there's nothing wrong with obesity, that fat is fine.

. . . The family member who avoids talking about a parent's drinking colludes with the alcoholic, tacitly agrees to uphold the fiction that the alcoholic's drinking is harmless — or that the alcoholic or addict suffers from fatigue and "nerves."

. . . The child who comes between a father and a mother as a confidante takes on an inappropriate adult role and creates a family intrigue that pits one parent against the other.

In each of these instances, the hidden aggressor, outwardly concerned and caring, encourages self-destructive behavior in the fellow-conspirator.

Sickness Tyrants

Rarely displaying anger, rarely exhibiting a desire for power and control, the sickness tyrant uses illness as a form of control.

The sickness tyrant usually comes from a family where parents were authoritarian or passive. Faced with threatening or inept parental models, the sickness tyrant never learned to express emotions directly, never learned to get attention through positive action. The sickness tyrant buried anger, felt futile and unimportant and powerless — **except when ill.**

Then people paid attention. Illness brought out caring

responses from others. After all, the sick person is not held responsible for being sick. So through infirmity, the sickness tyrant gets attention, feels important and powerful, and succeeds in controlling others.

Procrastinators

The procrastinator moves at a snail's pace, and thereby punishes others and stays in control. "I'll take care of it after a while," the procrastinator promises. "After a while" may be "in three hours." Or it may be translated into: "Tomorrow." "Next week." "Next month."

When the deadline nears, the procrastinator finds a myriad of excuses for being behind. And it's always someone else's fault. It's always outside the control of the procrastinator. The procrastinator's rule is: Blame others for being rushed, and continue to delay, continue to move slowly.

Late-Comers

There's so much to do, so many responsibilities . . . Quite naturally, then, the Late-Comer finds it impossible to be on time.

Not that the Late-Comer is intentionally late. Never! The Late-Comer spins out profuse and elaborate apologies, creative excuses. And all the while, the Late-Comer keeps us waiting, keeps others under control.

Chronic lateness can be an effective way to irritate, frustrate and humiliate others.

The Helpless

The helpless show weakness, fragility and tears — all the while avoiding personal responsibility and generating guilt in others.

The helpless one will drain the energy of everyone around. We see how fragile the helpless one is, how easily shattered by the slings and arrows of outrageous fortune.

We take care of the helpless. We protect the helpless. And the helpless one remains powerful through incompetence, weakness and successfully conveying frailty.

Low Self-Worth

I know of no sure way to judge what comes first — painful situations that produce low self-worth, low self-esteem. Or a personality heavily structured and weighted with low self-esteem that leads to further painful situations. But I am completely certain that low self-worth is part of a vicious cycle.

This is the vicious cycle: Low self-worth causes a person to behave in ways that are self-defeating, ways that produce negative feedback. Take John, for example. An insurance salesman, he seems caught in a self-defeating cycle. He suffers from low self-worth and is unsure of himself on the job. He communicates his anxiety and apprehension to potential customers and loses them. He's indecisive, and his job performance falters — which makes him feel all the more insecure and incompetent.

Cathy is caught in a similar cycle. She doesn't have very high self-esteem, so when she dates, she dates men who tend to treat her with little respect. They seem to be mainly interested in sex, and if she isn't interested, they're angry and sulk and never call again. If she is interested, they take her for granted — calling whenever they feel like it. Cathy finds herself in a situation where her low self-worth is reconfirmed and sinks even lower.

I am equally certain that growing up in an alcoholic family — or, for that matter, in any other kind of dysfunctional family — lowers the self-worth of the individuals in that family system.

All families fall somewhere on a continuum between painful, dysfunctional family systems, and healthy, optimally functional family systems. The healthier the family system, the higher the sense of self-worth. Similarly, the more painful the system, the more dysfunctional the family, the lower the sense of self-worth in each family member.

On the next page are some useful ways of looking at the relationship between healthy families and self-esteem of the family members.

Painful Family Systems That Lower Self-Worth	Healthy Family Systems That Build Self-Worth
1. No-talk rule	1. Communication is open
2. Internalized feelings	2. Open expression of feeling
3. Unspoken expectations	3. Explicit rules
4. Entangled relationships	4. Respect for individuation
5. Manipulation and control	5. Freedom highly valued
6. Chaotic value system	6. Consistent value system
7. Rigid attitudes	7. Open-mindedness
8. Reveres past traditions	8. Creates new traditions
9. Grim atmosphere	9. Pleasant atmosphere
10. Frequent illness	10. Healthy people
11. Dependent relationships	11. Independence and growth
12. Jealousy and suspicion	12. Trust and love

Obviously, troubled families are a prime source of feelings of inadequacy in family members — especially in co-dependents. Burdened with low self-esteem, co-dependents compare their outside appearances, achievements and expectations to other people — people who appear to be functioning much better than the co-dependent.

The co-dependent feels emotionally vulnerable. Hence, there is little true sharing of emotions within the family or with friends. Talk remains at a superficial level. Safe topics. Weather. The job. Chit chat about sports and hobbies.

Co-dependents live as if they are in constant preparation for some coming event — going to school, getting a job, marrying the right person, having a baby, making a living . . . in effect, co-dependents spend a great deal of time in getting ready to get ready.

The rehearsal is over. Life is here. And life is the performance. The busy business of getting prepared prevents the co-dependent from accomplishing small, achievable goals. And it feeds into the co-dependent's already low self-esteem and lowers it further.

Medical Complications

Walter Cannon, Hans Selye, and a score of other researchers have demonstrated the dynamics of stress-produced illness. The strain of keeping volatile feelings inside can contribute to physical illness in the co-dependent. In fact, there are many stress-related illnesses whose onset can be traced to a time of particularly high or acute emotional pain in the co-dependent.

And, more often than not, this pain originates in the family system.

What are some clinical clues that one very likely suffers from co-dependency? According to Dr. Charles L. Whitfield, associate professor of family medicine at the University of Maryland School of Medicine, the co-dependent may exhibit hypochondria, anxiety, depression, insomnia, hyperactivity, anorexia nervosa, bulimia, and suicidal gestures — to mention but a few of the clues.

In a similar vein, Dr. Max Schneider, past president of the California Society for the Treatment of Alcoholism and Drug Abuse, and former president of the California Medical Society, states that there are many diseases that commonly show up in co-dependents: Bowel problems, colitis, diseases of the respiratory tract, bronchial asthma, increased hypertension, and cardiac irregularities on a psychosomatic basis.

Dr. Schneider points out that emotion triggers our endocrine system, and we put out more adrenalin, more cortisone, and thus, in another vicious cycle, we increase cardiac arrhythmias.

Along with increased stress disorders, co-dependents tend to have many more fractures, burns, injuries and accidents. And co-dependents also experience problems with intimacy and with both sexual and non-sexual relationships.

Largely tied to hormone output, sexual performance can be impaired by emotional change, emotional stress. Frozen emotions, muddled emotions, supercharged and confused emotions — all can blunt one's ability to perform sexually.

The final health risks, of course, are suicide or murder.

Stages of Co-Dependency

"How do you know whether someone is just having a short-term bad time — just going through normal ups and downs of living — or whether they're seriously co-dependent?" It's a good question because many of the features of co-dependency **do** resemble the ups and downs of normal life stress.

By examining the stages of co-dependency, however, we can readily see the difference between co-dependent behavior and behavior that occurs in response to the stress of everyday life.

Stage One: Dependent Bonding

This stage is pretty much universal. We all go through an early period of attachment to a person in our lives — a parent, a relative, someone close who offers comfort and a sense of security.

With the co-dependent, the attachment may seem perfectly normal at first. The love and involvement may have a symbiotic quality — it may be reciprocal and mutually beneficial. However, co-dependent love and involvement becomes more intense and one-sided, and develops the characteristics seen as the stages of co-dependency progresses.

Stage Two: Fear

When one realizes that a dependency is developing — perhaps a one-sided dependency — one experiences a panicky feeling, a fear of loss and separation. Simultaneously, the co-dependent begins to realize that he/she has no ability to control the loved one.

The co-dependent then develops other fears — fear of abandonment, fear of loneliness, and fear of authenticity — the co-dependent becomes fearful of being a responsive person.

Stage Three: Emotional Paralysis

Fearful of losing the loved one, the co-dependent becomes emotionally frozen. "If I don't get angry, then Harry will love me and won't leave me, won't abandon me."

After a time of "stuffing feelings" and avoiding the pain of expression, emotional paralysis sets in. The co-dependent loses the ability to feel spontaneously. Joy and delight atrophy.

Stage Four: Behavioral Stuckness

Eventually, "stuckness" becomes the hallmark of the co-dependent. Feeling extremely vulnerable, the co-dependent person assumes fixed behavioral stances, protective defenses, repetitious, ritualistic patterns of behavior.

Features of stuckness appear in one who is disabled by chronic, mysterious illness. The workaholic and the compulsive gambler also display the kind of fixed behavioral stances, the ritualistic stuckness of the Stage Four co-dependent.

Other examples: The smoker. The glutton. The anorexic-bulimic. The compulsive shopper and clothes horse. And of course, the person who becomes addicted to alcohol or other drugs.

In Stage Four, the co-dependent loses the ability to be objective about his/her life, loses the ability to step back and see clearly what is happening — the stuckness, the self-destructive rituals, and the ever-present incapacitating fear.

INTERVENTION

Intervention with the co-dependent is difficult. But it becomes necessary. As difficult as it may be to intervene in the disease process of an alcoholic, it is often much easier than intervening with a co-dependent person.

Co-dependents, grown rigid and inflexible, have belief systems that are hard to penetrate. Co-dependents have habitually become controlling in relationships and have a great deal of difficulty in establishing intimacy.

It's hard for the co-dependent to surrender, hard for them

to say, "Yes, I see now what I'm doing. I see how I'm making my life unliveable, unmanageable. What can I do about it? How can I change?" Sometimes the "I know" stage is the last stronghold. Knowledge without action is the greatest self-con of all.

The tragedy is that co-dependents not only strongly resist change in themselves, but they are unwilling to let others get well. The co-dependent makes up excuses for the alcoholic, minimizes the problems, spins out rationalizations.

Confronted with hard facts, the co-dependent person counters with, "Yeah, but . . . Yeah, but . . . Yeah, but . . ." Indeed, "Yeahbut" might be called the distinguishing cry of the lost and woebegone co-dependent.

Despite the obvious difficulties, intervention with a co-dependent **is** possible. It's very similar to intervention with an alcoholic. Here's a brief outline of what's needed for intervention with a co-dependent:

1. Two or more caring persons — four to six would be ideal — who are willing to follow through, to be honest about what they see in the co-dependent's behavior.

2. Each of the intervening persons must also be willing to undergo formal training and education about the illness of co-dependency.

3. Specific data must be accumulated about the self-destructive behavior of the co-dependent. Collecting this kind of information may be more difficult than gathering data for an intervention with an alcoholic, because information about drinking tends to be more specific. For this reason, it is imperative that those concerned about the co-dependent get as much information and education as possible so that the data can be clear and unequivocal.

Data can be collected on the co-dependent's behavior, especially:

• Preoccupation: wondering what others are doing; wondering what others are feeling; wondering if they will get angry; unable to act independently without checking with others; afraid of being rejected by others; acting to get approval from others.

• Compulsive behavior: overeating, undereating (starving), overworking, over-spending, smoking, compulsive sex, shopping binges.

• Denied feelings, such as anger, hurt, loneliness, grief, fear, inadequacy — and the concomitant denial of tender feelings, such as affection, love and warmth in friendship.

• Helplessness: an inability, aversion or incompetence at dealing with everyday details of life, such as finances, seeking and finding employment, learning new tasks that expand one's knowledge and control of the world — in short, a stance that makes one heavily dependent on others for support and basic survival.

4. A suggested treatment plan, well-formulated and oriented to specifics, must be an essential element in the intervention. Otherwise, the process degenerates into a bitch session in which nothing is accomplished except ill-will and the development of stronger resistance in the co-dependent.

5. And, finally, there must be very clear consequences for the co-dependent, if the offered treatment is refused. Without some form of leverage, the prospects for a successful intervention are minimal. Few co-dependents will jump at the chance to change chronic, self-protective habits, because it will "be good" for them.

Here's how Connie handled an intervention confrontation with her sister, Janet:

"Janet, you have wanted to go back to school for the past three years, right?"

"Yes, but . . ."

"I know all the excuses. Now what I want you to do is to just listen to what I say — no interruptions. Okay?"

"Well, all right, but I've told you over and over why I'm stuck."

"Right. You've kept yourself from getting out of your rut by staying here in this small town because you keep hoping that Dan will get serious about your relationship. It looks to me like you are afraid to make a move on your own, so you keep waiting for Dan to make **his** decision to marry you, and then all the uncertainties will be solved. Yet, nothing in the relationship has really changed in the past three years."

"Well, no . . . but I don't think you should blame Dan. It isn't his fault!"

"I'm not blaming Dan, Janet. I'm not blaming anyone. I'm really worried because you've told me that you're hurt and angry, and yet you don't want to tell Dan how you feel. I love you, Janet, but I really don't want to listen any more to the stuff you should be telling Dan. You're letting yourself fall apart over this — you're edgy and irritable, you've gained at least 25 pounds in the past year. You're smoking — what — two packs a day now?"

"Sometimes two, and it's only 23 pounds — I'm not that bad."

"Maybe not, Janet. The question is — How bad do you have to get? How bad do you want it to get? I'm really worried about you — worried about where this is leading you. And I'm worried about your health."

"It sounds like you just want to bitch at me, like everyone else."

"No, Janet. I know it's tough, and I know you feel frightened and confused. I don't want to make it any tougher for you, but at the same time, I can't stand by and watch you continue to make it tougher on yourself. Unless you discuss your feelings with Dan, and take some action on your behalf, I cannot continue to be your 'listener'."

"Oh, Connie, I really want to. But I'm afraid. What if he — ?"

"What if he gets his dander up and rejects you totally?

Well, if he does, then maybe you've learned that Dan isn't really the kind of guy you'd want to hook up with. But if Dan really cares for you, that won't happen, especially if you bring the subject up in an honest way and without a lot of emotional intensity."

"I don't know whether I can do that — I get so angry."

"Sure you can. The first thing to do is think it through, and then practice. Come on, I'll help you."

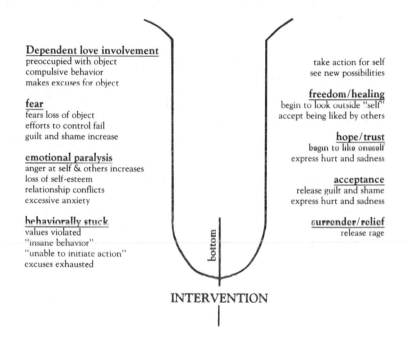

Dependent love involvement
preoccupied with object
compulsive behavior
makes excuses for object

take action for self
see new possibilities

fear
fears loss of object
efforts to control fail
guilt and shame increase

freedom/healing
begin to look outside "self"
accept being liked by others

emotional paralysis
anger at self & others increases
loss of self-esteem
relationship conflicts
excessive anxiety

hope/trust
begin to like oneself
express hurt and sadness

behaviorally stuck
values violated
"insane behavior"
"unable to initiate action"
excuses exhausted

acceptance
release guilt and shame
express hurt and sadness

surrender/relief
release rage

bottom

INTERVENTION

Chronic Conditions	Stages of Illness	Stages of Recovery
1. Stuck relationships	1. Dependent love involvement	1. Surrender and relief
2. Workaholism	2. Fear	2. Acceptance
3. Eating disorders	3. Emotional paralysis	3. Hope and trust
overweight	4. Behaviorally stuck	4. Freedom and healing
anorexia		
bulimia		
4. Hypochondriasis		
(multiple non-specific		
body complaints)		
5. Psychosomatic Illnesses		
ulcers, migraines, colitis,		
arthritis, gastritis		

Co-Dependency and the Dry Drunk Myth

For many years, recovering alcoholics and workers in the field of alcoholism have used the term "dry drunk" to describe a condition from which many sober alcoholics seemed to suffer — rigid, negative behavior, hostility, depression, dissatisfaction, and so on. In short, the phenomenon has been labeled a "dry" drunk because the behavior of the recovering alcoholic resembled the behavior of the alcoholic when drinking.

In other words, the sober alcoholic was on a drunk, but a perplexing kind of drunk, because there didn't seem to be any alcohol involved.

There have been many explanations of the "dry drunk syndrome," ranging from psychological conflict and immaturity to pre-relapse syndrome and the continuation of an unhealthy lifestyle in recovery — smoking, inattention to nutritional needs, over-consumption of coffee and other drugs, and inadequate exercise.

There is probably some truth in all of these explanations. But I firmly believe that what many times appears to be a "dry drunk syndrome" is simply undiagnosed and untreated co-dependency.

In recent years, clinicians who specialize in co-dependency have begun to spot the recovering alcoholic co-dependent and to provide treatment for the co-dependency. And clinicians have been excited and gratified to see the alcoholic co-dependent respond to appropriate treatment and leave the pain of co-dependency behind.

As founding Chairperson of the National Association for Children of Alcoholics (NACoA), I have had the pleasure of seeing a blending of alcoholics, spouses, and adult children in the membership of NACoA. The common denominator has been sharing the condition of co-dependency and forming support groups to help each other get well.

I have discussed this unusual blending of alcoholics, spouses and adult children with many medical colleagues, and several of them have suggested that the term "symptom re-emergence" might apply. It is just possible that the person who grew up in an alcoholic or painful family system was suffering from chronic co-dependency.

Somewhere the co-dependent learned to medicate the emotional pain of co-dependency with alcohol or drugs. Or to numb the pain by getting preoccupied with work or food. This medication, this numbing process progressed in the manner of addictions, until a primary addiction emerged. While the addiction progressed, however, the co-dependency lay dormant.

Here's where symptom re-emergence comes in. If an intervention took place, and the addiction was successfully treated, the co-dependency might still lie dormant. For a while. Then, as the chemically dependent person recovers with a focus **only** on the addiction, the co-dependency now re-emerges. The old emotional pain now returns, but it continues to go undiagnosed.

"But the co-dependent went through treatment for chemical dependency. Wasn't that enough? Why didn't treatment 'take'?"

Answer: Treatment **did** "take" — for the chemical dependency. But treatment for alcoholism — treatment for chemical dependency — does not deal with issues facing the co-dependent. The co-dependent who's a recovering alcoholic must get treatment that focuses on problems of co-dependency as well as alcoholism, if the person is to experience full recovery from both illnesses.

Unfortunately, the recovering alcoholic in distress is encouraged to follow-up with more alcoholism treatment to deal with the "dry drunk syndrome." Many such individuals end up feeling increasingly inadequate and guilty about meager progress in recovery.

The fact is, we professionals have not adequately served the addicted co-dependent. And clearly the time has come for a more systematic approach to this issue, for more adequate and full assessment and treatment of co-dependency in the person recovering from chemical dependency.

Why have professionals been slow to address the issue of co-dependency? Could it have something to do with the fact that so many professionals themselves have a history of co-dependency? Let's look at an area where the "no-talk" rule has reigned supreme — the professional co-dependent.

The Professional Co-Dependent

In my work, I have frequently noticed the high incidence of co-dependency among professionals — among counselors, therapists and administrators who work in the field of alcoholism and other addictions. And I am not the only one who has noticed co-dependency among professionals. This observation has been confirmed again and again by my colleagues.

I first noticed professional co-dependency years ago when I discovered that many of the professionals who came to my workshops on co-dependency were first-born children from painful families themselves. I began to see the dynamics as they told their stories of "trying to help" the families they came from — their families of origin.

Many of their early years were spent trying to understand themselves and their family systems, and then trying to help others. The process of learning to help others was in many ways an attempt at self-help, a subtle and approved way of easing the pain and confusion.

There seemed to be an overwhelmingly large number of nurses, physicians, psychologists, social workers, family therapists, clergy, and other helpers who found their way into my training. As they related their experiences, I saw the familiar strands of co-dependency woven through their histories. Those who were willing to work through the first difficult stage of anger and denial became better equipped to follow through by taking steps to resolve co-dependency issues — via counseling, group therapy, or some other form of recovery.

These people — these helpers, now recovered from co-dependency — have become the educators, the clinicians, the trainers and the leaders in spreading the word about the very serious and prevalent illness of co-dependency.

There have been other professionals, however — too many others, unfortunately — who have been unwilling to look at their own co-dependency. And their own fear and denial has led them to minimize the concept of co-dependency in others. Worse: The professional co-dependent has often actively blocked efforts to provide help for other co-dependents.

Signs of an enabling or unrecovering co-dependent professional include:

- Lack of knowledge about the dynamics of co-dependency — and a disparaging unwillingness to learn about co-dependency.

- A fear of resistance in the co-dependent and the resultant eagerness to accept excuses, minimizing problems, avoidances, and rationalizations.

- A need for approval from the co-dependent and a personal uneasiness in confronting someone who acts fragile, hostile, upset or powerless.

- Wanting to be a "Professional Hero" and "help" the family, rather than be a realist and feed back to the family its own dysfunctional behavior. The professional wants to be a "good guy" or "good gal" — a role learned in the family of origin — and wants to be a "helper" rather than truly "confronting" the situation. A "good guy" or "good gal" is always there to provide support.

• Denial of the professional's own need for understanding and support, thereby falling into the myth of the "super-therapist," invulnerable to the stresses that affect ordinary humans.

• Over-extended and under-cared-for. Martyrdom, burned out in the line of duty.

Particularly damaging is the physician who repeatedly treats stress and related illnesses in adults and children by prescribing tranquilizers, but who never explores the possibility of problems in the home, never refers to a family therapist.

Similar damage is done by counselors, social workers, psychologists and psychiatrists who buy into archaic theories of treatment, and insist that education and insight and awareness are all that's needed to stop compulsive use of alcohol and drugs, or to deal with compulsive enabling and resistance.

[On the other hand, there's the counselor who sees *every* — and I mean *every* — disagreement with his treatment plan as a sign of enabling. This counselor is always right about everything, and those who see things differently are seen as obstructive enablers. This type of counselor is stuck in a controlling power trap.]

Members of the clergy who are themselves co-dependent also fail to recognize addiction and co-dependency as primary illnesses that require specialized care. In short, the professional co-dependent can be found in every helping profession, in every organization that deals with people. This shouldn't be surprising, because as everyone should know by now, addictions are scattered throughout society, and co-dependency follows addiction as night follows day.

Signs of an Enabling or Unhealthy Professional System

When we have come from painful family systems or relationships, and we have not had an opportunity to recover, we often carry these problems and issues into the workplace. Institutional co-dependency exhibits the following characteristics:

1. There is tolerance, and even promotion, of excessive co-dependency in staff members. Excessive workaholism is seen as a positive trait. Loyalty to the organization may take precedence over self care and care for one's other friends and family.

2. There is resistance to new information about the illness of co-dependency. There is strong denial of the importance of education on the subject. Resistance may take the form of caustic remarks, sarcasm, ridicule and other forms of disparagement.

3. The need for treatment of co-dependency is downplayed — especially the possibility that professionals themselves might benefit from working through co-dependency issues.

4. There is much use of excuses to delay or deny programming to deal with co-dependency problems. Lack of money. Lack of time. Lack of staff. These excuses all sound logical and rational. And they are all a form of denial. As C. Northcote Parkinson wisely observed in his *Law of Delay*: "Delay is the deadliest form of denial."

Institutionalized enabling can obviously have varied negative ramifications — consequences which impede the recognition of co-dependency in all of its manifestations.
  • Deans of schools may block courses on alcoholism and co-dependency issues.

- Executive directors and administrators of community treatment programs may sabotage family programming or children's treatment programs.
- Insurance carriers may not include co-dependency treatment in their coverage.
- Schools may completely ignore the needs of children of alcoholics.
- Treatment centers may give only token educational programming to families, rather than the extensive treatment that's actually needed.
- Even some self-help support groups discriminate against the co-dependent seeking fellowship and support.

In conclusion, I feel that we must, as professionals, examine what baggage we bring from our lives into our vocations, into our workplaces. We would never dream of letting a chemically dependent counselor work with patients or clients. We would scream bloody murder if a psychologist or a psychiatrist came to group therapy reeking of bourbon.

We must take an equally responsible stand with regard to the co-dependent employee.

Co-dependency is a newly-recognized, treatable condition. That's the bottom line. Initially, co-dependency is the normal response to an abnormal situation. However, it is also progressive, chronic, and characterized by denial, compulsive behavior, and emotional repression. Quite obviously, co-dependency needs further attention and research.

However, we do know that intervention can work. It can be spectacularly successful if carefully planned and executed. That's the good news about co-dependency.

And the good news about the co-dependent professional is that change is also possible. It takes new information, a shift in attitude, and an openness and willingness to change.

2

Young Children
of Alcoholics
(Para-Alcoholics)

*Nature wants children to be
children before they are men.
If we deliberately depart from
this order, we shall get premature
fruits which are neither ripe
nor well flavored and which soon
decay We shall have youthful
sages and grown up children.
Childhood has ways of seeing,
thinking, and feeling, peculiar
to itself; nothing can be more
foolish than to substitute our
ways for them.*

— Jean Jacques Rousseau

All Children Learn What They Live and Experience

The child who lives with judgment learns to judge.
The child who lives with hidden anger learns to manipulate.
The child who lives with abuse and aggression learns to fight
*   and abuse.*
The child who lives with guilt learns to feel one-down.
The child who lives with depression learns self-pity.
The child who lives with competition learns to be jealous.

But there are other truths about living and learning in childhood:
The child who lives with honest praise learns confidence.
The child who lives with respect learns courage.
The child who lives with unconditional acceptance learns to
*   accept others.*
The child who lives with honesty learns to be truthful.
The child who lives with benevolence learns to be fair.

These traits fit all children to some degree, and the degree of fit frequently depend upon birth-order. But, more important, the potentials of children become seriously warped and distorted in a painful family system.

First, let's take a brief look at birth order.

Birth Order: The Burden and The Opportunity

We all have one thing in common: We were children — we experienced infancy, childhood and adolescence. And whether we like it or not — whether we agree or not — we were influenced by our juvenile history. In particular, we were influenced by our birth-order, our place in the family, or chronological rank among our siblings.

In my experience in working with family systems and with co-dependents and children of alcoholics in family treatment, I have been impressed with the way birth-order imposes a life-role on us as children. I believe that this life-role becomes so accepted and ingrained that we often fail to discover our true inclinations and identities until much later in life.

For example, firstborn children and only children — especially those born to parents who were not happy with each other — exhibit an overconcern (sometimes a meddling overconcern) for the welfare of the family system. They grow up to be what I call "Alerts."

Alerts become the family caretakers. Alerts remember birthdays. Alerts make sure the doors are locked and the lights are out and all the appliances are off. Alerts see that there are always plenty of ice cubes.

Alerts plan family get-togethers. Alerts verify timetables for planes, replace the paper in the photocopier, take the best notes, and speak up to break the silence.

Alerts know Robert's Rules of Order and, with an air of natural command, call the meeting to order.

If we find Alerts who balk at responsibility, we can always get them to capitulate by reminding them that they are the best — always reliable, always capable.

And Alerts go through life with a nagging feeling of dissatisfaction, a feeling that they are not accomplishing enough.

Middle children seem to have a lesser need for approval. Some middle children tend to rebel against the hyper-responsible and perfect first-born, and behave in the opposite way. These rebellious middle children preserve a shaky sense of self-worth by being able to act in a way they see as being independent.

They become defiant. They may pull away from the family and reject family values. They find their own friends, and they define and work out their own lifestyles.

How does it work out for the defiant middle child, for the rebel, the alienated one?

The middle children I've observed often seem destined to go through life in a one-down position, in an underdog stance, always looking for some kind of validation out of the mainstream and never being quite able to find the sense of belonging they crave.

Other middle children just pull away, with almost no hope of ever feeling a sense of family, with almost no hope of finding a truly satisfying relationship. And never attaining a stable sense of self-worth. They do not actively rebel against the family. They do not hold the family in contempt, they do not vigorously dissent against the family's values. They just quietly try to find their place in the world.

Oftentimes, these children find great satisfaction with a project they take on. Or with a career goal. However, their greatest inadequacy continues to be an inability to make and maintain meaningful relationships. Consequently, the middle child suffers from a chronic sense of loneliness and a fragile sense of self-esteem.

And what about the last-born, the younger children? Someone's always coming before them, so the younger children have to find ways to count themselves in. They compete for attention with humor. They go to extremes to get approval, to be noticed, to be loved. And the price they pay is the fear and insecurity of wondering whether they'd ever be noticed at all if it weren't for all the effort expended to make others pay attention.

This brief sketch obviously does not do justice to the role of birth-order in human development. But I have gone into much more detail on the relationship between birth-order and co-dependency in my previous book, *Another Chance*.

There is a population of children who are in an extremely vulnerable state during their formative years. As a result, they experience a very real trauma. Their circumstances are specifically different from those of other children.

The vulnerable population? Children of alcoholics and co-dependents. They come in all sizes, shapes, colors and ages. They share an important common bond: Each has learned a strategy, a dysfunctional way to cope with the alcoholism or addiction that has crippled their family system.

I invite you to open yourself to the next few pages in a very personal way. I grew up in a family shattered by alcoholism. And I have chosen my profession in working with alcoholic or drug-dependent families, in exploring the dynamics of painful family systems. I know from experience that what you will read in the pages that follow has relevance far beyond the chemically addicted family. My observations apply to all painful families which have produced unhealthy systems of denial, behavioral compulsions, and repressed emotions.

Young Children of Alcoholics

Psychiatrist Timmen L. Cermak has studied children of alcoholics. He is one of the founding members of the National Association for Children of Alcoholics and president of that organization. He grew up in an alcoholic family.

In 1983, Dr. Cermak wrote:

Children of alcoholics outnumber alcoholics. While the number of Americans with at least one alcoholic parent is not known, the figure of 28,000,000 is consistent with the National Council on Alcoholism's estimate that 10,000,000 Americans suffer from alcoholism and alcohol-related problems. A recent Gallup poll found that 33% of Americans feel that drinking has been a cause of trouble in their families.

With such an enormous population at risk, we would expect to find substantial problems, even if the detrimental effects of having an alcoholic parent were minor and short-lived. We know now that the effects stemming from parental alcoholism are significant and occur **throughout the life span** *of the offspring.*

But what exactly are the detrimental effects of having an alcoholic parent? What are the consequences of growing up in an alcoholic family — consequences that may occur throughout one's life span?

Clinical social worker Tarpley Richards lists a few of the consequences:

• Children of alcoholics are at higher risk for developing alcoholism themselves.

• Children of alcoholics gravitate toward alcoholic marital partners.

• The majority of child incest cases take place in alcoholic homes.

• Children of alcoholics also have a high rate of learning disabilities, attempted and completed suicides, eating disorders (including anorexia nervosa and bulimia), and unhealthy over-achievement.

Richards adds, "The problems of most children of alcoholics remain invisible because their coping behavior tends to be approval-seeking, which is socially acceptable."

The Booz-Allen & Hamilton Report on Children of Alcoholics, commissioned by the National Institute on Alcoholism Abuse and Alcoholism in 1974, was a landmark study that drew attention to the neglected area of children growing up in alcoholic families. Here are a few significant findings from the report:

• Many women, themselves children of alcoholics, were attracted to men who resembled their alcoholic fathers, either weak, passive and dependent types, or brutal, abrasive, authoritarian types. Almost half those who married, married a person with a drinking problem.

• Older children simply spend a lot of time away from home. Some actually run away, if only for weekends. Others become heavily involved in outside activities. High academic achievement is a frequently-used form of flight. Children submerge themselves in school, books, and in work.

In his book, *The Patient with Alcoholism and Other Problems*, Ken Williams, M.D., observes:

• Almost 50% of children of alcoholics were attracted to and married alcoholics. Others experienced a confused sexual identity or promiscuity.

• The incidence of other major psychiatric problems in the immediate family of the alcoholic is unknown. However, the experience of many clinicians working with alcoholic families is that the incidence is higher than the norm. Even if the family member began with the healthiest possible psychiatric stability, living with an alcoholic family member has a debilitating and warping effect. Even a psychiatrically normal family member will likely need a recovery program of his/her own.

Willard O. Foster, with the National Institute on Alcohol Abuse and Alcoholism, presented his findings on children of alcoholics in a conference at Johns Hopkins University in the 1970s. Here's a summary of Foster's main conclusions:

Instability, divorce, separation, desertion and early death are frequently associated with parental alcoholism. The alcoholic finds it difficult to retain the same employment for any protracted period, and this problem may also entail more numerous geographic changes, upsetting the child's schooling. The rate of separation, divorce and desertion among alcoholic parents is disproportionately high.

In understanding how parental alcoholism influences children, it is important to ask: "What's happening to the parents during this process?" Typically, the parent, whether alcoholic or co-dependent, suffers from **denial**. For the parent, there is no excessive drinking, no alcoholism. There is no over-reliance on tranquilizers and "nerve" medicine, no drug dependency. There are no family problems to talk out, nothing to discuss. Deny, deny, deny.

A child who consistently watches the parents deny reality develops a kind of internal split: The child may agree with the parents' version of reality, agree with the parents' perceptions, the parents' denial. Or the child may live precariously in two realities — in the world of denial framed and defined by the parents, and in the real world, as seen accurately by the child, but necessarily strategically suppressed. Children may adapt in either way, but both adaptations prevent the child from experiencing the truth — the accurate, undistorted validity of the child's own reality.

Children interpret their experiences and fill in with fantasy and myth wherever necessary. They adapt to get their basic needs met, to survive. And they very often feel as if they are living two lives: The life they project, the public life, the life as seen superficially by others. And the life they feel, the inner life, unspoken and unspeakable.

This contradiction can make the child feel unreal. Or phony, fraudulent, deceitful. With the feeling of deception comes a sense of inadequacy and the fear of being found out. "They will discover the real me," the child thinks, "and they'll find out that I'm not what I seem to be. They'll find out that I'm really a bad person." The fears and doubts lead the child to redouble efforts to cover up. The pretense must go on at all costs, and the chinks in the armor must be patched well so that no one can get through to the child within, the real child, vulnerable and unworthy.

Rokelle Lerner, co-founder and president of Children Are People, Inc., in Minneapolis, has worked with young children of alcoholics for many years. She has contributed a great deal to our understanding of what young children of alcoholics experience as they grow up in a family where reality is systematically distorted.

Children get many contradictory messages, says Lerner. They feel a need to "hurry and grow up," take charge of things, act like an adult. And, at the same time, they feel pressure to "stay little," stay a child, don't grow up.

For a hurting family, a family that is debilitated by alcoholism, and has few sources of pride, having a child who acts like a "little adult" can be a status symbol — a sign that the parents are really doing their job well. The child who walks early, who talks glibly, who behaves with impeccable manners, who achieves and performs like a grown-up — this child is coveted and respected.

Parents reinforce the behavior of the "little adult" but, at the same time, they discourage the child from being a child. The child is not reinforced for expressing true feelings, for asking to have its needs met, for forming different value systems, for expressing an interest in independence. In short, the message is: "Behave like an adult, but stay a child, stay little, stay in your place."

Adult-like behavior, coupled with a child's emotions, produces stress and chaos in a child. Many such children grow up to be adults who feel as though they've skipped childhood altogether. They were so alert for signs of approval, so diligent in seeking that approval and so busy meeting the needs of parents, the little adults didn't have time to be kids.

Another complication: Alcoholic and co-dependent parents inevitably create an environment of emotional deprivation for the child. The chemically dependent parent medicates emotions, and they come out distorted: Anger becomes vicious, brutal rage. Love becomes maudlin sentimentality. Depression and anxiety become self-pity and suspicion.

The co-dependent parent, the spouse of the alcoholic, represses emotions. Anger translates into bitterness and long-seething resentment. Fear and anxiety show up in nervous disorders or physical ills.

Given these family dynamics, it is not too much to suggest that children growing up in an emotionally handicapped environment will, in their own emotional development, become emotionally handicapped.

Para-Alcoholic: Patterns of Adaptation

Jael Greenleaf, author of *Co-Alcoholic, Para-Alcoholic*, uses the term "co-alcoholism" to refer to the adaptive behavior of an adult, generally the spouse of an alcoholic, or someone who has a close relationship with an alcoholic.

Says Greenleaf, "The prefix 'co-' means 'with,' or 'necessary for the functioning of '." The adult who assists in maintaining the social and economic equilibrium of the alcoholic person is indeed co-alcoholic. The vast majority of alcoholic people are in dyadic relationships, whether it be with spouse, parents, lovers, or in some cases, a close friend."

On the other hand, Greenleaf uses the term "para-alcoholism" to refer to the **imitative** behavior of the children growing up in an alcoholic family.

"The prefix 'para-' means 'like' or 'resembling', " Greenleaf argues. "The child who grows up in a family with the alcoholism syndrome learns behavior from both parents and becomes para-alcoholic. In any consideration of etiology, parental role modeling and familial environmental structures are the primary sources of information."

Young children from alcoholic homes become, in a sense, para-dependents. Imitating both Mom and Dad, the para-dependent child acquires role model attitudes and habits from both the alcoholic parent and the spouse. And the child thus develops a chameleon-like personality.

Just as the chameleon changes color to blend into its environment, para-dependent children alter external behavior for protective purposes. They can laugh, smile, look surprised or serious in an instant. The exterior display —

READER/CUSTOMER CARE SURVEY

If you are enjoying this book, please help us serve you better and meet your changing needs by taking a few minutes to complete this survey. Please fold it and drop it in the mail.

As a special **"Thank You"** we'll send you news about new books and a valuable **Gift Certificate!**

PLEASE PRINT   C8C

NAME: _____

ADDRESS: _____

_____

TELEPHONE NUMBER: _____

FAX NUMBER: _____

E-MAIL: _____

WEBSITE: _____

(1) Gender: 1)_____Female 2)_____Male

(2) Age:
1)_____12 or under   5)_____30-39
2)_____13-15   6)_____40-49
3)_____16-19   7)_____50-59
4)_____20-29   8)_____60+

(3) Your Children's Age(s):
Check all that apply.
1)_____6 or Under   3)_____11-14
2)_____7-10   4)_____15-18

(7) Marital Status:
1)_____Married
2)_____Single
3)_____Divorced/Wid.

(8) Was this book
1)_____Purchased for yourself?
2)_____Received as a gift?

(9) How many books do you read a month?
1)_____1   3)_____3
2)_____2   4)_____4+

(10) How did you find out about this book?
Please check ONE.
1)_____Personal Recommendation
2)_____Store Display
3)_____TV/Radio Program
4)_____Bestseller List
5)_____Website
6)_____Advertisement/Article or Book Review
7)_____Catalog or mailing
8)_____Other_____

(11) What FIVE subject areas do you enjoy reading about most?
Rank: 1 (favorite) through 5 (least favorite)
A)_____ Self Development
B)_____ New Age/Alternative Healing
C)_____ Storytelling
D)_____ Spirituality/Inspiration
E)_____ Family and Relationships
F)_____ Health and Nutrition
G)_____ Recovery
H)_____ Business/Professional
I) _____ Entertainment
J) _____ Teen Issues
K)_____ Pets

(16) Where do you purchase most of your books?
Check the top TWO locations.
A)_____ General Bookstore
B)_____ Religious Bookstore
C)_____ Warehouse/Price Club
D)_____ Discount or Other Retail Store
E)_____ Website
F)_____ Book Club/Mail Order

(18) Did you enjoy the stories in this book?
1)_____Almost All
2)_____Few
3)_____Some

(19) What type of magazine do you SUBSCRIBE to?
Check up to FIVE subscription categories.
A)_____ General Inspiration
B)_____ Religious/Devotional
C)_____ Business/Professional
D)_____ World News/Current Events
E)_____ Entertainment
F)_____ Homemaking, Cooking, Crafts
G)_____ Women's Issues
H)_____ Other (please specify) _____

(24) Please indicate your income level
1)_____Student/Retired-fixed income
2)_____Under $25,000
3)_____$25,000-$50,000
4)_____$50,001-$75,000
5)_____$75,001-$100,000
6)_____Over $100,000

**NO POSTAGE
NECESSARY
IF MAILED
IN THE
UNITED STATES**

BUSINESS REPLY MAIL

FIRST-CLASS MAIL PERMIT NO 45 DEERFIELD BEACH, FL

POSTAGE WILL BE PAID BY ADDRESSEE

HEALTH COMMUNICATIONS, INC.
3201 SW 15TH STREET
DEERFIELD BEACH FL 33442-9875

FOLD HERE

((25) Do you attend seminars?
1)_____Yes   2)_____No
(26) If you answered yes, what type?
Check all that apply.
1)_____Business/Financial
2)_____Motivational
3)_____Religious/Spiritual
4)_____Job-related
5)_____Family/Relationship issues
(31) Are you:
1) A Parent?_____
2) A Grandparent?_____

Additional comments you would like to make:

_____
_____
_____
_____

Thank You!!
HCI
The Life Issues Publisher

The characteristics — traits, feelings and behaviors of Children of Alcoholics

The name of the game or the mode of survival.	What you see or Visible traits. Outside behavior.	What you don't see, or the inside story. Feelings.	What he/she represents to the family & why they play along.	As an adult without help, this is very possible.	As an adult with help, this is also very possible.
THE FAMILY HERO or SUPER KID.	"The little mother" "The little man of the family." **Always** does what's right, over achiever, over responsible, needs everyone's approval. Not much fun.	Hurt, inadequate, confusion, guilt, fear, low self-esteem. Progressive disease, so never can do enough.	Provides self-worth to the family, someone to be proud of.	Workaholic, never wrong, marry a dependent person, need to control & manipulate, compulsive, can't say no, can't fail.	Competent, organized, responsible, make good managers. Becomes successful and healthy.
THE SCAPEGOAT or PROBLEM KID.	Hostility & defiance, withdrawn & sullen, gets negative attention, **troublemaker.**	Hurt & abandoned, anger & rejection, feels totally inacequate & no/low self-worth.	Take the heat, "see what he's done" — "Leave me alone."	Alcoholic or addict, unplanned pregnancy, cops & prisons. TROUBLE. Legal trouble.	Recovery, has courage, good under pressure, can see reality, can help others. Can take risks.
THE LOST CHILD	Loner, day dreamer, solitary (alone rewards, i.e., food), withdrawn, drifts & floats through life, not missed for days, quiet, shy & ignored.	Unimportant, not allowed to have feelings, loneliness, hurt & abandoned, defeated and given up. Fear.	Relief, at least one kid no one worries about.	Indecisive, no zest, little fun, stays the same, alone or promiscuous, dies early, can't say NO.	Independent, talented & creative. Imaginative, assertive & resourceful.
THE MASCOT or FAMILY CLOWN.	Supercute, immature, and anything for a laugh or attention, fragile and needful of protection, hyperactive, short attention span, learning disabilities, anxious.	Low self-esteem, terror, lorely, inadequate & unimportant.	Comic relief, fun & humor.	Compulsive clown, lampshade on head, etc. Can't handle stress, marry a "hero," always on verge of hysterics.	Charming host & person, good with company, quick wit, good sense of humor, independent. Helpful.

the public performance — completely hides the hurt, anger, shame and loneliness within.

A divided self results: A self that gets approval and acceptance for being a chameleon, and a secret self, the inner person no one knows.

The basic characteristics of para-dependency are set down at a very early age, and these features — these characteristics of children of alcoholics — systematically interfere with adequate functioning:

- They see situations as black and white, all or nothing.
- They develop a pervasive mistrust of others, of life itself.
- They find ways to compensate for the guilt and shame and pain they harbor inside.
- They attempt to control others to protect and cover their fears.
- They do not recognize boundaries and become over-involved in the parents' business.
- They become so afraid of making a mistake and of failing that they sabotage any **satisfying** success.

As the child grows older, para-dependency becomes more sophisticated, more intricate. And more necessary. We'll take a closer look at older children of alcoholics in Chapter 4. Right now, let's examine several case histories of young children of alcoholics.

Cindy's Story

I met Cindy one day at the beach, She had sand in her eyes and she was staggering around on the beach trying to get the sand out. She was six years old. She was alone.

"Is there anything I can do to help?" I asked Cindy.

"No," she said politely, still rubbing her eyes.

"I can see that it must really hurt bad," I said. "Maybe if you could just cry, the tears would wash the sand right out."

Cindy kept on rubbing. She was groaning, but not crying.

After watching her agony for a few more minutes, I asked Cindy where I could find her parents. She told me that she was alone, and she seemed frightened that I might locate them.

Finally, Cindy consented to come with me, and I drove her to a hospital where the E.R. staff cleansed Cindy's still-tearless eyes.

After I wheedled and coaxed, Cindy gave me her telephone number. I called her home. Her mother was out, but her father answered the phone and swore, "What the hell is going on! She must have gotten herself in trouble at the beach. I'll be down to get her . . . but if she's crying, I'll give her something to cry about."

Later, when Cindy's father showed up, he was angry — very upset — and he was very drunk.

I met Cindy's mother at the hospital and asked her some questions about the family. At my suggestion, Cindy came into a program I had for young children. In the support group for children of alcoholics, Cindy finally divulged that she had stopped crying as an infant. Feelings weren't allowed in Cindy's home.

Later, Cindy's mother joined a group. And eventually I did an intervention on both Cindy's father and brother. They went to alcoholism treatment. Her mother went to co-dependency treatment and Overeater's Anonymous. Today, the whole family is in recovery.

Brad's Story

Brad was five when he came to group. He was a confident-appearing little boy. He came into group when his father went into treatment for alcoholism.

From the first, Brad had trouble relating to the other little boys who had learned to be honest about their sadness and feelings of hurt, and their feelings about being isolated and left out at home. Over and over, Brad said that he had plenty of time with his father, and that they really had a good time together.

When finally pressed by the other boys in his group to tell them more about his relationships with his parents — especially with his father — Brad explained, "I have plenty of time with my dad. Every Saturday my dad sits down in his big brown leather chair to watch sports on TV. I sit with him."

The other little boys told Brad that just being together does not mean you are close to your parents. What did they do together? What did they talk about? Where did they go together? What games did they play?

Brad shrugged and went on with his story. "I watch my dad. He usually drinks two six-packs of beer. I always wait until he drinks at least one. Then I watch for something exciting to happen on TV. When it does, and my dad gets real excited, I run over and turn off the TV. Then my dad jumps out of his chair and chases me around the house. He always catches me 'cause he's lots bigger. Half the time he messes up my hair and says I'm a cute little devil just like he used to be. The other times, he beats me up. Sometimes I have a bloody nose, and once he cut my lip." Brad stopped and was silent for a moment. Then he solemnly added, "But he catches and holds me, every single time."

Janet's Story

Janet was 13 years old when she came to group. Janet was overweight and felt unattractive. She had a hard time expressing herself. It was difficult for Janet to talk about her own needs, and it was weeks before she shared any feelings at all. She preferred to smile enigmatically and to bring treats for the rest of the group.

On Easter week, when the kids had a vacation from school, the group decided to have a slumber party at a summer cabin owned by the parents of one of the girls in the group. Janet was more excited than I had seen her since she first started coming to the group. Everyone in the group made plans to go.

The next week Janet came to group in a sullen mood. She explained that her family would not give her permission to go on the slumber party outing. Janet's parents planned to attend an A.A. convention that week, and they felt that she needed to go with them.

Janet was disappointed, discouraged and heartbroken. She had waited so long to become truly part of the group . . . and now this!

But the rest of the group members rallied and offered a possible solution. Perhaps, we suggested, Janet could sit down and tell her parents how important this cabin party was to her. She could make her needs known, and seeing how strongly Janet felt, her parents would surely relent, would surely change their minds.

The next week Janet came in even more sullen. And ashamed. And guilty. She made her needs known, all right, and when she did, Janet's parents told her that they were ashamed of her for feeling as if **her** needs were as important as **their** recovery. After all, Janet's parents reasoned, they had an illness. And this convention was part of their recovery. And Janet should be happy that they were working on their program.

Janet brought donuts for everyone.

There are thousands of stories like Janet's and Cindy's and Brad's. The children all have different names and the stories have slightly different variations, but the underlying themes and issues remain constant:

Lonely, sad, and hurting children in alcoholic families, in desperate need of attention, love and understanding.

More than a hint of the anguish can be seen in a poem written by a children's counselor as she held a two-year-old child beaten by a drunken father:

ABANDONED

When I heard your helpless cries
Tears began falling from my eyes.
I read you books
You gave me looks.

Your big brown eyes
Showed pain inside.

Your heart must moan
From being alone.

How could you understand
A raging father's hand?

How can your little mind
Justify brutality so unkind?

I wish I could make you see
You don't have to fear trusting me.

You cannot possibly understand
That my heart is in your hand.

I hold you close, your tears subside
My feeling for you I cannot hide.

I only wish that I could heal
The confusion and suffering that you feel.

Thank God you are a child
Innocent, forgiving, trusting, mild . . .

My mood is down, my heart is broken
For my feelings suppressed — unspoken.

The world holds frustration, hate and rage
But WHY for a child of your age?

I pray your future holds love and cheer
A world of happiness to replace the fear.

I hope I touched your mind and heart
To give your world of love a start.

Because inside I died
When I held you while you cried.

Anonymous

Is there a way out for the kids living in alcoholic homes? Claudia Black, Ph.D., thinks so. A founding member of the National Association for Children of Alcoholics, Dr. Black has written extensively about young children of alcoholics. And her description of the universal message sent to children of alcoholics is recognized nationwide: "Don't talk. Don't trust. Don't feel."

However, she believes that we can give children living in an alcoholic home some essential "basic messages" to counteract the universal message. It doesn't take a professional or an expert to convey the basic messages, says Black. It just takes an individual willing to bring up a touchy subject in a caring way.

The crucial messages for children in alcoholic families are:

• Tell the kids they are not alone, they are not unique weirdos or freaks. Let them know that at least one out of every ten kids will have a parent who drinks too much.

• Help the kids understand that they're not to blame for their parent's addiction.

• Explain about chemical dependency in terms that they can understand, that the addicted person is sick and can't easily quit drinking or taking drugs.

• Convey hope by letting them know that the addiction is treatable, that there are many ways for the alcoholic or drug-dependent person to get assistance.

• Let them know the importance of taking care of themselves, of taking care of their own needs, and point them in the direction of whatever recovery source exists in the community — Alateen, Al-Anon, or groups set up especially for children of alcoholics.

Barbara Naiditch and Rokelle Lerner, co-founders of Children Are People, in St. Paul, MN, have contributed a great deal to our understanding of young children of alcoholics. Their pioneer work in school systems has been invaluable and it is worthy of emulation on a broad scale.

As Lerner and Naiditch and others working with younger children of alcoholics have learned, intervention with the alcoholic very often fails to meet the needs of the young children. Treatment programs, focused primarily on the alcoholic and the spouse, have been excruciatingly slow to recognize the need for treatment of youngsters as well.

We have found in our work with para-alcoholics that youngsters do indeed recover. They find ways of getting in touch with the submerged self. They find ways of expressing their needs and getting them met.

Here's a fragment of a 15-year-old boy's quest for recovery:

I HURT

Have you ever hurt really bad. . .
Something has made you so very sad
My heart has cried itself out and sometimes
*   cannot stop.*
There is that awful feeling when you look and
*   meet eyes*
A picture that you cannot lose
And yet you will live in your mind all your days.

It's a man who can hardly walk
He meets your eyes and yet he doesn't talk
The skin once tan is now yellow

The body strong is now older and slower
Alcohol is taking his life away.

As you look at him you shake inside
You cry inside and are polite outside
It's a feeling, one you cannot share
The safe world you used to know now is no more.

You look at this man you have known all your life
And you really know him no more
You cry because he gave you your life
You even get angry at God.

This man I saw as I passed him on the street
I looked so close and saw my own dear daddy
I've asked him to stop this thing
But something stronger calls from within.

God, take care of him, and God, please
    bless his heart. . .

In a group with other youngsters from alcoholic homes, this boy moved from a surly and defiant stance toward his father and was able to articulate his pain. The poem represents an awakening, as the youth found his hurt, found understanding of his father and found forgiveness.

Here's a letter I received from a 16-year-old girl — a letter that vividly shows the conflicts facing children in families torn apart and scarred by the chemical dependency of a parent.

Dear Ms. Wegscheider:
    Thank you for coming to my high school. I learned a lot and now need more information. This condition has been in my family for as long as I can remember. It never struck me as unusual until recently.

*My mom is on medication for her back. She is on medication all the time. It is easier to let her take the pills than to listen to her complain **all the time**. I realize that sounds cold, but to live with her is torture!*

She is suicidal and we found that taking the pills away made the pain "unbearable" and she'd attempt suicide.

*My father works nights and sleeps most of the morning. He and I do the cleaning, he does the shopping. My mother has absolutely nothing that she **has** to do. She has many hobbies to occupy her time.*

All we do is fight when I'm around her, so I stay away most of the time. I know that leaving her is not the right answer, but there is no sense in forsaking my sanity too. I've been having my own problems to deal with. Her loss of memory drives me crazy. She asks me a question five times a day. Doesn't know what day it is, sleeps so much, she sometimes doesn't know whether it's day or night. She never knows when she took her last pill.

She uses 14 different kinds of pills. I would appreciate any information, if it's not too late.

> *Sincerely,*
> *Cathy*

Was it too late for Cathy's mother? Too late for Cathy? Almost. Cathy attempted suicide between the time she wrote this letter and the time I received it. Thankfully Cathy survived.

I helped Cathy find a support group at a nearby Air Force base. She got help for herself. Unfortunately there was no way to intervene with her mother or father. Cathy, however, got the encouragement and support she needed and was able to finish high school. Cathy made it, but her parents continued in their illness.

In the next chapter, we'll hear from another child from an alcoholic family in more detail, from her early years into adulthood. We'll let Sharon tell you her story, and her story is **MY STORY.**

3

My Story:
One Child
From An
Alcoholic Family

My father was an alcoholic. It took many years for me to be able to admit that my father drank, that his drinking was not only self-destructive, but also nearly destroyed my family. It took many years for me to understand that my father suffered from the disease of alcoholism.

During his lifetime no one in our family would have called him an alcoholic. I grew up in a small town, a rural community, population 600, where the term "alcoholic" was never used. We used euphemisms and synonyms, but we never labeled a heavy drinker an "alcoholic."

Instead, we said: "He drinks too much." And a person who drank too much . . .

- really gets loaded;
- was flying high;
- was schnookered, blasted, looped, tipsy.

And, of course, it was easy to see that the drinker was "feeling good, feeling no pain."

There were winos, town drunks, and bums. But we never called anyone an alcoholic.

My Family

At times my family was a joy. I thought I could never be happier. We had picnics, parties, much food, and good times. But we also had bad times, times of anger and bitterness, times of fear and confusion. And, like most people, I experienced moodiness and periods of intense loneliness.

Whenever a friend would ask my about my family, I would eagerly talk about the joy, the pleasantries. And I would keep the bad parts, the miserable experiences, hidden inside. I could not reconcile the good times with the bad times. I couldn't understand the inconsistencies in my family, the wild swings from happiness to despair.

Consequently, I felt confused . . . deeply confused.

The Good Times

Living in a small town meant that my family knew almost everyone in town. And everyone knew us. I grew up surrounded by people and activity — never a dull moment. To me, the drugstore was a bazaar of fascinating trinkets, baubles and exotic perfumes and colognes. It was the only place in town you could get a genuine cherry phosphate soda, a drink that sparkled on your tongue and tickled your nose. And the drugstore had a comic book bin where you could browse for hours over the latest amazing exploits of *Superman* and *Wonderwoman* and *Submarine Man*, and, of course, *Batman and Robin*! The drugstore also had a fashion shop devoted to all the mysterious paraphernalia of womanhood.

The town boasted a movie theater where we noisily reveled in the Saturday afternoon matinees. At intermissions we converged on the mechanical marvel — a popcorn machine . . . on wheels.

There was a post office with "Wanted" pictures of fugitives and desperadoes posted on the wall. There was a telephone switchboard with an operator who placed the calls, a hospital, gas stations, and a community hall.

My father owned a major business in this town, and our family was respected by the community. We fit in. We belonged. I was proud of our little town, and sensed that other people in our community were proud of my family, proud of me.

I was a first child and also a first grandchild. I have felt special since I was a little girl. My father told me over and over, "Sharon, you are special, very special, and you can do anything."

My aunts and uncles liked having me visit. And my relatives took an interest in my schoolwork and my extra-curricular activities. Time and again they came to watch me act in school plays. And when I debated or participated in oratory and public speaking contests, my relatives were a supportive and sympathetic audience. I felt that they took a real interest in me, that they cared about what I did. And I felt I could rely on them.

I spent a lot of time with my grandma in my early years. I was her special first grandchild. And she taught me about the warmth and love of God, and I grew up with a deep faith and trust in a Higher Power.

My family and friends liked to have a good time — liked games, special occasions, parties. My dad played softball and in the summer the whole family would go to the games to watch him play. Of course, there was always lots of cold beer at the ballgames and after the games, but, as all the players said, it wouldn't be a ballgame without the beer.

We also had an annual Fourth of July family shindig, a big family party. We'd go to a nearby state where fireworks were legal and we'd buy several hundred dollars' worth of firecrackers, cherry bombs, sparklers and rockets. Then we'd set up a fireworks display at my uncle's farm, and the **whole town** would come for a spectacular evening of slightly illegal pyrotechnics. There was always drinking, but the drinking seemed like part of the social occasion.

And we spent hours around the piano, playing and singing. It was our home entertainment center. Grandma played by ear, and I read music. Each Sunday afternoon we had a sing-along, and we laughed and joked and sang old familiar melodies and some of the newer tunes. My father's favorite was "You Always Hurt The One You Love." I still have the sheet music.

Sundays also meant Sunday dinner: chicken or roast beef, potatoes and gravy, homemade rolls — and always a couple of extra places set at the table for friends, for company. My mother was a fantastic cook, and my mouth still waters at memories of Christmas candy, potatoes and old-fashioned gravy and home-made cinnamon rolls.

During family get-togethers my dad played host, seeing to it that everyone had plenty to eat and plenty to drink. He'd see to it that plates were heaped, glasses well-filled. "Have some potatoes," he'd urge. "Better have another helping of those peas and carrots." And, after dinner, dessert — homemade pie or cake or cobbler. He heaped generous portions on every plate. Dad grew up in a family of want and need, and he wanted to share his prosperity.

My early years were quite happy. With my family, I especially remember being touched with affection, respect, and love. I remember a soul-warming sense of comfort.

Yet, even at this time, even when I felt happy and content, I also felt at times an underlying sense of uneasiness. And I didn't know why.

I didn't tell anyone. It was as if I wore a veneer of serenity — all smiles and charm and conviviality. But inside my heart would pound furiously and I would tremble with fear. But I didn't know why.

My parents did things I couldn't understand. Sometimes my dad would be irritable over small things — a tear in the screen door, a new scratch on the car fender. He seemed pressured and he'd get madder and madder. Enraged, he'd yell at Mom or me. Or at my brother. Dad would start blaming, as if it were important to establish once and for all who was responsible for every peccadillo. This started when I was about 12 years old. I felt like I'd been bad, unspeakably bad — like I'd done something terrible and disgraced my father. I never understood the reasons for his angry behavior.

When we had company, when friends or neighbors visited, my family seemed to be together, seemed to be amiable and cordial and happy together. But when friends left, the facade lifted, the amiability and happiness vanished, replaced by tension and anger and tears. My mother cried a lot. And I felt trapped in strange, uncomfortable emotions. But I couldn't tell anyone, not even my closest friends.

When I was five years old, I ran away from home again and again. I remember being found in a neighbor's attic. Another time my parents found me hiding out in the cemetery. I recall wandering, alone, down the aisles of a train. But they always found me. They always brought me back.

I ran and ran, but I don't remember what I was running away from.

I also recall the discomfort and nausea of car-sickness whenever I left home, especially if, for one dimly comprehended reason or another, I was being sent away to stay with relatives.

Running. Escape. Inside I wanted to run, and yet I didn't want to leave. I felt alone, empty, sick. I wanted someone to hold me, to listen to my innermost fears and conflicts.

And yet, when I was around those I loved most, I felt physically ill. Desolate and uncomprehending, I prayed for help.

Tired and defeated, I started to miss school. I played "sick" about once a week in my early school years. Grandma would then make a fuss over me and I'd get lots of love and attention. The nights were the worst times. I could hear my mother and father arguing. ". . . money . . ." ". . . too expensive . . ." "bills . . ."

There was a lot of tension about finances. But there was an even stronger undercurrent of bad feelings that came out when they argued about their relationship, the lack of closeness my mother felt, and her yearning for more time together. My dad would end up yelling. My mom would cry. And I would cover my head, and I would pretend not to hear. But I couldn't avoid the noisy confrontations. I shuddered when the clamor started, and my stomach knotted up and ached. I used to make up my own world, a place where it was pretty, quiet and safe. It felt good to lose myself in reverie, to have a fantasy world of my own making, where no one ever worried, or argued, or cried.

The Elementary School Years

In grade school, I found a way to escape. I worked hard. I did everything my teachers asked. They liked me and praised my compliance, my eager and industrious attitude toward schoolwork. I learned to read early, and I did my assignments promptly. I wasn't a dawdler. I was always good with words and I was religious. In Catholic grade school, I had nuns as teachers. Sister Beatrice paid special attention to me when I felt down, when I was troubled by homelife, but couldn't talk about it. She'd tell me, "Sharon, you have great talent and determination. You'll manage in this life—you'll manage and survive."

Sister Beatrice told me, and I believed her. I flourished in school. The teachers' praise felt good. I worked hard, did everything they asked — and more — and they praised me. I learned that if you work hard, do things right, people will like you.

My teachers obviously liked me. The neighbors liked me. My friends liked me. And my life seemed to smooth out. When things were better for me, I also felt better physically.

At the same time, there was a lot of drinking going on at home, but the attitude was that drinking was normal and anyone who didn't drink was abnormal.

I didn't think much about it. I had other interests, other preoccupations. I found ways to keep busy. I started taking pictures with my Brownie camera and putting them in scrapbooks. I bustled around doing housecleaning to help my mother. And laundry and ironing.

Then there were school projects and church activities. I grew up Catholic and the church played a very big role in my life. I loved the structure of Catholicism, the consistency. The Church taught me trust and predictability. Later in life, some of my early learnings came to seem rigid. Yet in the early days, the Church provided a haven and planted an enduring belief that God would be the most consistent factor in my life.

I could handle the days. I knew how to fill the hours. The nights, however, continued to be frightening. When my parents came home angry after an evening of drinking, I could hear them bickering and yelling in the kitchen or in the bedroom. "I don't care what happens!" my father would yell, as they quarreled about money, about family problems, or about sex. But I wanted so much to believe that everything was O.K. — that we were one big happy family day and night — that I never told anyone what I heard.

Even if I heard doors slam and furniture fall heavily to the floor, even when I found my mother weeping on the couch — I pretended not to see or hear.

The next morning, life went on as if nothing had happened.

Yet, inside I was terrified. What was happening? I was overwhelmed with feelings of loneliness.

Why doesn't anyone tell me what's going on?
What's going to happen?

During the day, I had lots of fun with my dad and my brother and my sister. Especially Sunday afternoon. We went for drives to visit neighbors and to see the countryside. We went on picnics, played horseshoes, joked, planted a garden, played the piano and sang songs.

I didn't have much fun with my mom. She always seemed to be working or tired. But I loved her, and I helped take the pressure off her at home by doing housework, cleaning, helping with the cooking and other chores.

I tried to make her happy, tried to make her proud of me. And I always went to my mother for solace and comfort. She met other needs, too. There was very little money in the house, and my mother kept a band-aid box with silver coins for all my emergencies.

I had fun with my dad, I felt secure with my mother — and all the while, I felt so lonely. I had no one to tell my feelings to.

Teen Years

When I was 14, my family suffered a severe crisis. My father's business was destroyed by fire. Our whole existence was threatened . Money was scarce enough before the fire, but after the fire the family income looked hopeless.

I was terrified. No one was talking, no one was trying to lessen my fears. Mom and Dad talked with each other, but they didn't tell me anything. "Don't worry," they'd say. "Don't worry."

Don't worry. I would lie in bed and wonder whether we would have enough food. Would I ever get to go to college now? What would happen if my parents had heart attacks from the strain and worry of this crisis?

Don't worry. I worried about everyone — my parents, my brother and sister, my grandma. I wanted to help and I didn't know what to do. I felt guilty for being another burden. I felt angry because other kids seemed so secure. It wasn't fair!

I cried myself to sleep night after night. But I never told anyone about my worries and fears. Daylight hours were for making people happy.

Becoming A Family Princess

I hit upon a way to help the family, to mitigate the crisis and, at the same time, to become less of a burden. I'd become financially independent.

I found jobs. I worked for my father — did bookwork for his business. I also did bookwork for a gas station. Whenever I could find the time, I took baby-sitting jobs.

I paid my own expenses. And I bought things for members of my family. Out of my earnings, I bought a beautiful copper lamp for my mom. I bought clothes, toys, and books for my brother and sister. Once I bought my sister a red sweater set and I was proud of how cute she looked. I tried to buy the extras for our home. Financial independence relieved some of my guilt, but my contribution was so small that I continued to feel very inadequate.

At the same time, I noticed changes in my father. He started leaving home at 5:00 a.m. to open his business. At around seven, he would give me a ride to school. I could smell alcohol on his breath when he picked me up. But I never mentioned it to anyone.

After school I would stop to see him at work, just to say "hello" and to see if he was okay, or if there were errands to do. Almost always I could smell the alcohol.

In the evening, Dad would often go to sleep on the couch. The rest of the family moved in stony silence through the house.

The changes I saw in my father increased my fear. He didn't talk with me as much as he used to. He didn't seem interested. There were few jokes, very little laughter, and no joy at all. The music had gone out of our lives.

Dad seemed angry all the time — angry and grouchy, like a wounded bear. Fearful of his temper, I told him only the good things, because he might lose his temper and blame me if everything in my life wasn't just so . . . perfect.

I feared my father, yes, and I also felt sorry for him. I thought maybe he drank because of the fire. Or maybe it was because of the war — WWII. He went into the service when he was still suffering from the effects of a car accident. He was in combat in Germany, got wounded in action, and had a problem with his leg that lasted for years. (As a small child, I used to walk down to the river and throw flowers in the water, truly believing that my father would get them in Germany.)

Or maybe Dad drank because he never knew his parents. He had a hard life growing up as an orphan. His own father was an alcoholic, physically abusive to his family. Dad's mother abandoned him and her other kids when Dad was seven years old. He was "farmed out" to relatives who raised him. I felt he never had a chance, and that life had treated him unfairly.

I decided to make up for losses, failures and set-backs he had suffered. He deserved more out of life, and I would see to it that he got the respect and recognition that he deserved.

I wrote to "This Is Your Life," a popular television show hosted by Ralph Edwards. Each week a guest of honor listened to a stream of warm recollections from people in the past who really cared. Long-dead memories were stirred, old friendships were renewed — and everyone could see that the guest of honor was a worthy person. It was just what my father needed.

I was desperate. I wrote an 18-page letter begging the producers of "This Is Your Life" to select my father to be a guest of honor. I waited with high hopes. But as the weeks went by without a response, my hopes faded. I never received an answer, not even a form letter expressing regret.

No matter. If "This Is Your Life" wouldn't honor my father, I'd honor him myself. I'd make him proud — so proud of me! And if he was bolstered by pride, then maybe — just maybe — he wouldn't have to drink.

I worked harder at making friends and collecting honors, friendships and honors bestowed, indirectly, upon my father.

I won two state oratory contests.

I was president of four high school clubs: Library Club, Future Homemakers of America (FHA), Spotlight (school newsletter), Girl's Athletic Association (GAA).

I was an honor student, a member of the Honor Society.

I received the American Legion Award, given by the American Legion to the high school student who demonstrated leadership, integrity, accomplishment, trust and commitment.

And I was a Homecoming Princess.

What honors for Emil! Relatives would come from hundreds of miles to watch as Emil shared his daughter's honors — to watch Sharon, Homecoming Princess, ride triumphantly down Main Street with a retinue of homecoming royalty.

My father would be so proud, I thought. We'd laugh and talk together once again. **And the drinking?** Ah, yes, the drinking would . . . go away.

By the time I got home from the homecoming parade, my father was celebrating my accomplishments, celebrating with booze. And within an hour, he was drunk and passed out.

I was pained, angry, and disappointed. I felt helpless — helpless and thoroughly humiliated. That night I cried myself to sleep without changing my homecoming gown.

And what about my mother during these years? My relationship to Mom was full of anger and guilt.

I was angry because she didn't work things out with Dad. Maybe if she were different, he'd be different. Maybe she was putting too much pressure on him. Maybe she didn't give him enough love. Maybe . . . maybe . . . maybe.

At any rate, I was getting tired of being Miss Perfect, tired of having so many responsibilities. I worried about who was going to take care of Dad when I left home.

Would she try to make him happy? Or would they just fight and hurt each other. Anger swept through me as I thought about Mom. And then I would be filled with guilt and remorse.

How could I be mad with someone who was obviously suffering so much herself? Mom worked so hard — she had to put up with so much. And through it all, she took such good care of everyone. I was ashamed of the bitterness I had felt toward her.

But I also decided that I didn't want to be like her. I didn't want to be the kind of woman who worked hard for everyone else and took nothing for herself. I didn't want to be a patient, uncomplaining person. I wanted something out of life myself, but I felt guilty and selfish about meeting my own needs.

As usual, I kept all these feelings inside. **No one will understand**, I thought. Besides, I had my image to protect — my image, and the image of my family.

It was hard to keep my true feelings and thoughts to myself. Once in a while I would slip. Often when company came to dinner on Sunday, the grownups would carry on long conversations as we ate. As I grew older, I began to have my own opinions, my own ideas on a wide variety of subjects. When I expressed my ideas, my dad would disagree. It wasn't the disagreement that hurt, it was the sarcasm he showed, the disrespect, the put-downs. Sometimes he would insult me and belittle me. If I fought back, he got angry. If I cried, I was accused of being too thin-skinned, too sensitive.

I never shared my feelings with either of my parents alone.

Most of my outbursts took place at the Sunday dinner table. If my father disagreed with what I said, or if my words displeased him, he would retaliate by insulting and embarrassing me. Then I would feel humiliated and end up in tears. No matter how hard I tried to hold them back, the tears would come.

"You're nothing but a cry-baby," my father would say. "You're too thin-skinned. Can't take a joke."

Sometimes I fled in tears to my room. Other times I would be forbidden to leave the table, and I sat silently weeping before a plate of cold food.

Only once did I dare to speak back. "It isn't fair!" I cried. "It isn't fair for you to insult me just because I have feelings! I think that's wrong, and I think you're being cruel when you make fun of me whenever I say something. You think you're being funny when you ridicule me—well, it isn't funny!"

And only once did my father ever slap me. I stood in shocked disbelief. Here was the man who

> loved me . . .
> hugged me . . .
> protected me . . .
> taught me to drive . . .
> taught me to do bookwork . . .
> taught me to dance . . .

Here was the man who took me to ballgames and sang when I played the piano . . . and he slapped me because I dared to tell him truly how I felt.

I learned a profound lesson about how to cover up my feelings with those I loved. I learned that it was dangerous to be honest about my feelings.

And increasingly, emotional pain was becoming a part of my everyday life. It was no longer the nights that hurt, no longer the nights alone that were filled with fear and loneliness, with worry and pain. My emotions churned day and night.

Young Adult

I wanted to leave home, wanted to find a way to escape the growing turmoil. Yet I didn't dare go. Who would take care of my family if I left? But I was graduating from high school — that made it acceptable to go. Most of the rest of my graduating class were leaving to get jobs or go to school. Graduation resolved my dilemma. It wouldn't be acceptable to leave if I **wanted** to, but it was acceptable for me to leave because **everyone else was doing it.**

Four days after graduation, I left home and moved to a city 100 miles away. It felt good to be away during the week. I was very old for my years. When I now look back, I sometimes feel as if I were born adult, a grown-up, somehow absurdly encased in a child's body.

Away from home, I was capable and found it relatively easy to manage my own life Monday through Friday. For the first year, I went home almost every weekend to make sure everyone was all right.

My family appeared to be getting along well — on the surface, of course. But I could sense the tension, the old familiar stress and hints of pain. Tight lips, sharp glances, strained smiles and lackluster cheerfulness — all contradicted my parents' earnest assurances that everything was "just fine."

Everything was not just fine. But I didn't push it. I was so in need of relief myself that I wanted to believe in the facade, I wanted to take the pretense as face value. I was too tired to probe — too tired and too wary.

I was also enjoying my first real taste of freedom. But my pleasure with new-found freedom turned out to be short-lived. I began to feel guilty once more, guilty about the worsened conditions at home, and the impact on my brother and sister. I knew from the outstretched arms of my little sister that she was lonely for me. My brother's stuttering and the tears in his eyes told me that he was hurting and needed comfort and a haven.

There was an overwhelming sense of deterioration at home. The house needed attention and repair. My mom's once-beautiful flower gardens were overgrown with weeds. The paint was chipping off the house, and the house itself seemed to be wearing out. The roof leaked, the drains clogged with increasing frequency, the ancient wiring was dangerously overloaded.

My mother was aging rapidly and suffered frequent, often inexplicable illnesses. My father wore a glassy-eyed vacant look, as if he were mesmerized by a vision of a bleak and joyless future.

Each time I returned to the city, my father wept and told me of his love for me. I will always remember him, tears streaming down his face, as he waved good-bye from the front porch.

I started getting sick when I went back to the city. Terrible stomach pains. High anxiety. Finally I was hospitalized with acute abdominal pain.

After peering and poking and probing and running many tests, physicians made a diagnosis: Physical and emotional exhaustion. I spent several days in the hospital, and when I was released I was ordered to spend two weeks in bed.

During this time of chronic stress, I had been working full time as a private secretary. I also belonged to a dance club, took voice lessons, belonged to a bowling team, worked as a volunteer for the Big Sister organization . . . And I found time to go out on dates two or three nights a week. Not a single person in my Monday-to-Friday life knew about the family turmoil that ensnared me, entangled me from a distant 100 miles.

I led two lives for Sharon, and my secret life was every bit as covert as the undercover life Herbert Philbrick led for the FBI. I had my pride and self-worth to protect. But I paid a price in weariness, in physical and emotional debilitation.

And there was more guilt. I felt guilty about my independent life, ashamed of enjoying the pleasure of dancing or bowling. How could I be out having fun when my family was in pain? Prayer, trust and hope were all that kept me going during this time.

Bed rest. That's what the doctor ordered. Naturally I spent most of the time thinking about my family. I resolved that I would try once again to make things better. "Only this time it will be different," I told myself. "I will take better care of myself."

A small, still voice in my head timidly asked, "How?"

I ignored the voice. "I will be strong and I will make things different for my family," I told myself, building up a hollow kind of confidence.

The small still voice persisted. "How? How will you make things better, Sharon? Are you really sure you can handle this?"

"Of course I can," I muttered. "I will just have to work harder and try to keep from getting emotionally involved."

Brave words. Perhaps I should have listened more closely to the still, small voice.

But I did work harder. And I took better care of myself. I took surprise gifts home. I gave a big surprise birthday party for my dad. I bought presents for my sister and brother.

I also became engaged, and my parents made plans for the grandest wedding our community had ever seen. All the relatives on both sides of the family were coming.

There was a sense of gaiety surrounding my wedding plans. There was fun and laughter once again. Music. Food. Animated conversation.

Maybe things would be like they used to be. Maybe our lives would be close once more, and all the fear and guilt and anger — all the unhappiness and insecurity would vanish like a bad dream. I felt excited and I was filled with anticipation.

My father bought cases of liquor for the wedding party. I begged him not to serve it.

He looked at me in sheer disbelief. "What kind of a wedding party is it that doesn't serve liquor to the guests?" he argued.

But I was firm. "I won't come to the party if the liquor is served," I told him. I did not want my wedding to be spoiled, as I knew what would happen after the liquor began to flow.

We made a deal: No liquor during the day — only in the evening at the party. A small, but important victory for me. It ensured at least that the wedding itself would not be spoiled by my father passing out as he gave the bride away.

I asked for help from a friend who hid my car in her garage. After the wedding, and before the party, my husband and I made our getaway. I knew that it was more important for my father to serve liquor than it was for me to be at my wedding party.

Wife and Mother

My free time was now taken up with new roles: A wife, a social butterfly, and a homemaker. And I was pregnant for the first time. But I felt good about my marriage, good about imminent motherhood. My mind was filled with exciting plans and preparations. It was a stimulating time, a sunny, zestful time.

I found that I made friends easily and enjoyed social life — vacations. I was congenial, good-humored and cheerful. It felt good to build a new life. I appeared happy, I enjoyed having fun and meeting interesting people. But no one really knew me well.

Sometimes I'd go home for holidays or birthdays, but I began to go home less frequently, and I put more and more energy into my own life. I devoted my time to making a home away from home. After all, my home now was with my husband. I loved my new home, my own space, my friends.

Yes, it felt good to be away from my family. All the guilt and shame I felt about this was buried deep inside.

When my son was a baby, six or seven months old, I felt that since he was their first grandchild, my parents deserved some special time with him. We went for a week-end, but I decided we'd spend the whole week. It had been a long time since I had spent any longer than a week-end with my parents.

I immediately regretted my decision to stay a whole week. All my worst fears of earlier years were confirmed. And then some. My father drank constantly. He didn't appear drunk — didn't stagger around, didn't slur his words or laugh long and raucously at inappropriate times — but he had that old familiar rigid, glassy-eyed, vacant look. My mother was sick and she cried a lot, even though she tried to hide the tears. Her face was tired and drawn. She looked aged far beyond her years.

My father was mean and insensitive to my brother. My father had unrealisitic expectations . . . there were familiar insults and put-downs again, only this time directed at my brother. And my brother was trying to act like a growing young man, cool and indifferent. He'd shrug and pretend it didn't hurt — yet I knew that it did. I could see and feel the pain in his eyes.

My little sister was a bundle of nerves. She was shy and uncommunicative. And when she did speak, there was tension and anguish in her voice.

Three days had gone by — only three days — and I couldn't stand it! I wanted to pack up my baby and get out of town as quickly as possible. In desperation I called Donald, a friend with whom I had gone to school. I begged him to come and get me and drive me back to the city, back to the safety and sanity of my husband, my own home.

It was the middle of the night, but my friend said he'd come. Very quietly, I began to pack up my clothes and my baby to sneak out of my parents' home. Sneak. I had to get away undetected, because I knew how much my father loved me and his grandson. It was a strange kind of love because my father couldn't tell the difference between love and possessiveness. Everything and everyone he loved had been taken from him — his mother abandoned him, his father died an early alcoholic death, his business burned.

I knew my father would never let us go.

I quietly crept down the stairs when I saw headlights outside. As I was going out, the baby started to cry, and my father appeared almost instantly.

He ordered me to stay. "If you take that baby and leave now," he warned, "you'll never be welcome in this house again!"

I tried to tell him how I felt, but he wouldn't listen. He had been drinking. He was hurt and angry that I was so afraid. He screamed at me. He told me I had broken his heart, if I truly believed that he ever meant to hurt me or the family.

As he screamed at me, I screamed back. "Can't you see what's happening to everyone? Mom's sick. My brother's confused and has no one to turn to. My sister's almost a nervous wreck. I just can't take it any longer!"

My sister now peeked down from the top of the stairs. My brother was on his way down to help me. My father grabbed him and threw him down. My mother was there sobbing, and my son was screaming in my arms. It was an ugly scene. I thought I would go crazy.

I ran for the waiting car, ran as if I were fleeing for my life. Then we were on the road, away from the madhouse, away from the family. We drove fifty miles in silence, and then, acting as if nothing unusual had happened, I asked my friend to stop at a phone.

I called home to check on my family. I was afraid my father, enraged by my flight from home, might lash out at the ones I'd left behind. What if he killed my mother? What if he blindly lashed out and killed my brother and sister?

Thinking these horrid thoughts increased my guilt, but I couldn't help it. My worry was real, and I needed to know if my family was still alive.

My mother answered the phone and relief surged through my body. She told me not to worry. I apologized for being such a problem for them. I was sorry, I said. Truly sorry. I hung up in tears.

This was my turning point.

Once a tower of strength and determination, I was beginning to crumble. I was weary, burnt out . . I was no longer the family caretaker. I was no longer the one who'd fix things so that the problems would disappear.

I was fast becoming the family problem myself.

From Special Caretaker To Problem

I became pregnant again, and the first three months of my second pregnancy I was very ill — sick enough to be bedridden most of the time. I suffered from migraines and ulcers, as well as anxiety and depression — now easily recognized as stress-related disorders. There were times I was so incapacitated — so physically run down — that my doctor had to examine me at our home. I was simply too weak to go to his office.

My mother discounted my infirmity. "You don't know what being **really** sick is," she'd say, as if she'd cornered the market on authentic illness. Of course, mother was always sicker and more in need of help than I was, so I kept quiet about most of what was happening to me. And I tried to avoid contact with her, because each time we got together, each time we spoke, a resurgence of guilt swept over me.

My solution? **Draw back, Sharon, draw back from the family.** I couldn't handle the turbulent emotions generated by my parents' demands, by my father's drinking and my mother's chronic infirmity. I needed a respite from pandemonium. Once again I pulled away from my family.

It helped. But about once every three or four months, I would cry. A release, a release of pain — fear and grief. Quiet tears at first. Then huge wracking hysterical sobs. Eventually the tears would stop, or the family physician would give me a shot that would put me to sleep and end the weeping. Then I would be strong again . . . for a while.

My daughter was born in the fall of the year. Another time of excitement: A granddaughter for my mother and father! Just the thing to help reconcile the bad feelings between me and my father.

My mother and father planned to visit us and the two grandchildren for Christmas Eve. All day we waited eagerly. Then it was evening. They were late. Something **had** to be wrong. They had called early in the morning and confirmed that they were coming. But my mother's voice was low, strained and guarded. It was the kind of voice that came following a big family fight.

As time slowly crawled on, Christmas Eve lost its rosy glow of cheer and fellowship. The carols, the baubles, and the presents seemed ominous, foreboding.

About 7:00 p.m. my uncle called. He simply said, "Your dad died. He was a good man. It wasn't his fault. Come home."

My mind went numb. **Dead**, I thought. **Impossible! He's only 46 years old. He can't be dead! Must be a car accident.**

I left my babies with friends and began the 100-mile-drive to my parents' home. I expected to find my family and their car wrecked along the road. I didn't.

As I pulled up in front of my parents' house, I saw a bedraggled Christmas tree in the front yard. I was to find out later that in a fit of anger my father threw it out the door earlier in the day.

Dazed, almost like a zombie, I went in. Tear-filled voices came at me in a jumble, and I pieced together fragments...**Dad was drunk that morning...family fight...noon...mom, brother, sister...had to get out, went to visit...relatives in the afternoon...Dad... alone...committed suicide...must have been afternoon, late afternoon.**

The words began to jell in my mind. Dad, drunk and alone, had committed suicide. I heard the words, but I didn't want to believe them. I wanted dad to come down the stairs and put his arm around me and tell me that everything would be all right.

Everything was not all right, and it wouldn't be for a long, long time. The next ten days were filled with tumult, with horror, shock, and grief, with anger, hurt, and fear — and above all, confusion and the nagging thought that if only I had been there . . . If, if, if . . .

Family Caretaker Returns

I mustered up strength. I comforted my sister and brother. I helped my mother, helped her clean out my father's business papers. Helped her write thank you notes to friends and relatives. Went with her to open my father's safety deposit box and found that the house and cars, which had been paid for, had been secretly mortgaged by dad for drinking money.

I mustered up strength. I kissed my father good-bye. He was wearing the navy blue suit he bought for my wedding. I ran my fingers through his curly black hair — the hair I had loved so much as a child. I studied his face. Familiar, so familiar, but I would never see it again, except at moments when I see the family resemblance in my image in the mirror, or when my son laughs and holds his head a certain way. **There's Dad**, I say to myself. **There's Dad.**

I was in control throughout it all, the detailed arrangements, the funeral, the aftermath. I hurt, I grieved inside. But I didn't cry. Sharon shed no tears for Emil.

After ten days I went home, home to my husband and babies. I was afraid that my old family life would drag me away from my new family, that old family ties would sap my strength and take me away from my new friends.

I told everyone, "My father died of a sudden heart attack." And, "Yes, it was a great shock. A great shock."

Caretake To Problem: II

Once again my life began to crumble. I was swamped with work and demands. My two babies needed a good deal of care, energy and time. I was just 24, and my closest friend was the same age. And she was dying of cancer.

My husband wanted my time and energy too. He urged me to let go of my family of origin. My attention belonged to him and the children, he told me. My new family needed all of Sharon, not a fraction of Sharon left over when she had time. My husband and family needed a healthy, vibrant Sharon, not an ailing Sharon, not a distraught wife and mother full of nameless fears and anxieties.

I felt torn and pulled and pressured. And then another call came from home. Six weeks after my father's death, my mother herself was on the verge of death. I was called home again. Sharon would take charge.

During the next few days, I made arrangements for mother to have surgery. I helped my brother and sister get set up in alternate living arrangements. And I scurried around the house making sure it was tidy and secure and that the lights and water were shut off. Finally, I returned home to my babies.

I cared for my children during the day, and made the 150-mile trip in the evening to be with my mother until she got out of intensive care.

I was drained, and I felt myself getting sick again. I felt myself becoming emotionally numb. And I felt a growing sense of dread. I was desperately afraid of loss and anxious about my own guilt. There was a bitter irony in love, I thought: **Love? If you love something, it will be taken away.**

My children. My husband. My mother. My best friend. I loved them all — would my love bring them unhappiness? Would it end up killing them? A superstition, perhaps, but I was frazzled and vulnerable, flooded with anxious thoughts, worries, and even superstitions when it came to those I loved.

I was afraid my mother would die, that my children would get hurt, that my house would burn down. I dreaded the thought that I would get ill. "If I get sick, who will take care of everyone else? Who will do what needs to be done? Who will do Sharon's job?"

A few short weeks after my mother's surgery, my best friend died. I sat up comforting her husband all night. We were all so young. She hadn't even got a good start in life, and she left a two-year-old son.

I went to the funeral home the next day to say good-bye. I returned to my own home and started to cry. This time I could not stop.

Deeply depressed, I cried for days. I could no longer escape, could no longer run, hide and cover up. I could no longer pretend.

"It will be all right."
It will not be all right!
I could no longer muster up strength, I couldn't be strong. This was my bottom. I could do no more . . .

I was hospitalized for depression. I refused medication. I could feel the relief of the tears, a kind of blessed relief. I did not want to stop crying. I just wanted to feel. I wanted to grieve. I wanted to stop — stop hurting, thinking feeling, trying, struggling. I wanted to stop **living.**

On Becoming A Choicemaker

As I hit my own emotional bottom, as I considered suicide, I knew that something had to change or I couldn't survive. After what seemed like an eternity of weeping and grieving, I surrendered to the one constant source of strength and hope that I knew to be real. I asked God to take me into His care and somehow put me back together again. I prayed and prayed. And I waited.

The answer came back to me: "Make choices. Love. Trust. Change." The message was loud and clear.

I decided to fight back. I decided to survive.

Then began the slow, painful process of becoming emotionally honest with myself. I had to find out what my own needs were. Then I needed to be honest with others about my needs.

My needs! No more evasion, no more pretense, no more martyrdom. I had to take a look at what Sharon needed for a change.

It was scary. And it didn't happen overnight. Sharon had a great fall, and there were no King's horses and no King's men to put Sharon back together again. There was no magic fairy godmother who'd wave a sparkling wand and reassemble all the shattered fragments of Sharon's psyche.

The process was instead difficult, painful, and sometimes surprisingly wonderful and delightful. I did not always like it, but I slowly gained understanding.

I went back to school. I had always been good at school, and I had often regretted giving up a four-year college scholarship and going to work instead. Now I appreciated school.

In my third year of college, an alcoholism degree program opened up in Minneapolis. I jumped at the chance to learn more about this illness.

In a few years, I completed a B.A., a master's degree, and a chemical dependency certification program. I had always been an achiever.

I made two other major decisions. I got a divorce, and I took part in a therapy group.

Divorce! "My God, you don't really mean you're going through with it!" one of my friends gasped in disbelief. Divorce was the kind of thing you might think about, you might ponder it, or even casually mention it to a friend. But it wasn't something that a conventional young woman did — it just wasn't proper!

What was proper? It was proper to stick together for the children's sake. It was proper to stick together for security. It was proper to endure a relationship that just didn't mesh because it was humiliating to admit failure in marriage.

Yet I went ahead with the divorce.

My mother rejected me for taking such a drastic step. My children reacted with baffled anger and resentment. My friends let me know clearly that they disapproved. Yet I went ahead, for I did not want to stay married for my mother's sake, or for my children, or for my friends. I felt this was the first major life decision I had made for myself, and it brought me a great deal of pain. It was an important decision. Over the next few months and years, I learned I could survive.

I also learned that sometimes you know inside what is right and necessary. I was beginning to believe in myself and starting to trust my inner knowing.

With that first major step taken — divorce — it became easier to take subsequent steps. There is a Zen saying: "When the student is ready, the teacher appears."

Part of the process of change included professional treatment — I was treated as a child from an alcoholic family system. It felt good to have someone hear how I felt for a change — how **Sharon** felt. And it felt good to have someone tell me I was okay. "Sharon is a good person." I liked the sound of it.

My teacher appeared in the person of Gene Burke, a priest who facilitated a therapy group. I learned a great deal from him about "**possibility.**" I had felt trapped for so long that I had grown to believe my helplessness — my powerlessness and my limitations. With Gene's support and encouragement, I began to act in my own behalf and feel good about it.

For many years, my teachers and mentors were also the children, young adults and adults who came to my first counseling center, "The House," in Minnesota. I wrote at length about "The House" in my first book, *Another Chance*. Hundreds of us gave each other mutual support and encouragement as we explored thoughts and feelings — as we learned that we were, in fact, more alike than different. We learned that we weren't crazy and alone, that we weren't odd creatures full of bizarre emotions and wicked thoughts. We had normal feelings, given our tension-filled and shattering life histories. And we learned that we could grow to become Choicemakers, open to change and transformation.

I began to be able to separate the disease of my parents from the people my parents were and are. With that ability, I became able to separate my behaviors and illness from who I was. I began to love and respect myself in a new way.

The way to fully accepting myself and growing to love myself truly has been hard at times. Hard? At times, it seemed well-nigh impossible. During the years, there have been many more hurdles, including the growing prescription pill addiction and alcoholism of my mother. However, I had acquired some tools to work with. And most important: I now knew that treatment was readily available for alcoholism and chemical dependency, and no one needed to suffer needlessly from this disease.

With the help of other professionals, I arranged an intervention with my mother. One of my greatest joys was when my mother asked to be taken to the treatment center, where I also went into treatment with her as her child — an adult child of an alcoholic.

The healing between us was miraculous. I have a deep sense of pride in my mother — pride in the courage it took for her to go through treatment, pride in her determination to recover from her addictions. And I have pride in her ability to let go of the past, to take each day as it comes.

One of the difficult problems I've had to face over the years is that just as the child fears the parents, the adult child fears authority. As I tried to bring my personal experience to my work as a professional, I met with a great deal of rejection. Working with families was outside the mainstream of psychology and social work, on the far fringes of social services. After all, the argument went, there was an "identified patient" to deal with — the alcoholic or chemically dependent person. Once the alcoholic was "fixed" the family would run good as new. In a sense, the identified patient was a lot like a faulty carburetor — a malfunctioning mechanism that could be overhauled — or even replaced — without affecting the performance of other parts of the car's engine. The analogy was a mechanical one, oversimplistic and insensitive to the organic interconections in a family system.

It was a long, lonely struggle to try to bring family systems theory to bear on family problems. Professionals balked and treatment centers complained that they had all they could do to deal with the alcoholic, much less the family.

Recovering alcoholics were afraid that they would be reminded of the old pain in the family, and they didn't want to become aware of unfinished family business, because it would be another stress to deal with in recovery.

Spouses and family members didn't want to see themselves as being part of an illness-system. It was the **other** person who was sick, who was the "identified patient." Spouses and family members were reluctant to seek their own therapy, reluctant to make changes. It is always more comfortable to believe that the alcoholic or drug-dependent person is at fault.

Children, too, wanted to avoid. They were tired of continued chaos in the problem-centered family. Kids found their own survival in fantasy, or outside the family. They simply didn't want to feel the hurt, guilt and anger that came from facing their own roles in family hassles.

Because so many children of alcoholics become attracted to helping professions, many untreated adult children are in professional positions offering services to the chemically dependent or to families. Adult children are conditioned in youth to giving service, taking care of people, trying to figure out relationships and trying to understand themselves and others. Naturally, then, they gravitate to care-taking professions — to nursing, teaching, counseling, psychology, medicine, clergy, and so on.

Untreated for their family illness — scarcely even aware that a family **can** be afflicted — these adult children in the helping professions still suffer from their own resistance to the family illness concept. To accept that information fully would be making an assessment of self, would be admitting that the helping professionals themselves have wounds that have not healed, have sedulously-guarded areas of vulnerability. It would mean admitting that even professionals themselves need help in dealing with the family issues growing out of the family illness of chemical dependency.

Fortunately, recent developments have made it easier for helping professionals to recognize their adult child status, and at the same time it has become more acceptable for helping professionals to take steps to resolve their own unfinished business.

In February, 1983, Joan Kroc invited several people to the Kroc Ranch in Santa Barbara to discuss the needs of children of alcoholics. Along with several of my peers in the field, I came ready to share my expertise, experience and knowledge.

As we introduced ourselves and began talking about the gut-level important events that had shaped our lives, an unusual intimacy developed among us. We had come together as virtual strangers to one another, and in our uncannily similar experiences, we discovered we were soulmates. We had the kind of instant understanding that's extraordinarily rare and precious. The meeting had an indescribable quality of holiness.

Members of the group who attended the meeting at the Kroc Ranch became the founders of The National Association of Children of Alcoholics (NACoA).

On my way home from the meeting, I reflected on what had taken place the past few days. I wrote a letter on the plane to my new NACoA friends and colleagues:

Dear NACoA Friends,

As a child who grew up in a family suffering from alcoholism, I have struggled with the fear and mistrust of feeling a sense of belonging — of joy and hope. As many of you know, my father died an alcoholic suicide at the age of 46. My mother suffered for years with pill and alcohol addiction. They were warm and wonderful people and parents; it was the alcohol that devastated our family.

I spent half a lifetime in what felt like struggle — too many ways to mention here. There were highs and lows, losses and gains — but never much relief from the feeling of struggle. What was constant through all this, however, was the ability to feel a Higher Power and to know at some level that I belonged as a child and servant of that Power. The hope and joy was transmitted through people caring, and that care has nurtured and sustained me. Each of you reading this letter knows who you are and your relationship to me.

Through people and my Higher Power, I have accomplished some things I'm proud of. The births of my three children were events of total ecstasy to be equalled only by the intensity and commitment I felt in their growing years.

As I sit on the plane flying from California to Texas, I am allowing myself to experience the awe and humility I feel right now. I feel that the birthing of NACoA and its need for commitment and nurturing are important values for me and for each of us.

In the speed of what has happened in the 48 hours just behind us, I was a "good CoA" [child of an alcoholic], full of task and purpose. It is only now — alone — that I am flooded with feeling . . . As I look down on the mountains, it feels right. I'm flying high. What my tears are saying for me is:

I am honored that you want and trust me with the role of Chairperson for your national organization — one that I believe will make a difference in the world of alcoholism and addiction. I sincerely feel "joy, hope and a sense of belonging." To serve and work with the caliber of people who sat in on this historic formation meeting was enough good feeling to last a long time. To be able to continue in a role of trusted leadership is an honor.

I pledge to help each of you expand in whatever way you want, with respect to serving the organization; and I will share with you whatever *talent and gifts I have in order for us to work together as a collective body of people "who care."*

Together, we will bring hope to thousands who still feel "crazy and alone."

Sincerely and with gratitude,
Sharon Wegscheider

NATIONAL ASSOCIATION FOR CHILDREN OF ALCOHOLICS
Front Row left to right: Cathleen Brooks, Tim Allen, Tarpley Richards, Barbara Naiditch, Mary Brand. Second Row: Sharon Wegscheider, Bobbie Hodges, Jael Greenleaf, Robert Ackerman, Phil Diaz. Third Row: Robert Subby, Patricia O'Gorman, Timmen L. Cermak, Julie Bowden, Herbert L. Gravitz. Not Shown: Stephanie Brown, Claudia Black, Ellen Morehouse, Charles Whitfield, Joseph Kern, Rokelle Lerner.

Today, NACoA is a fast-growing organization, and concerns about children of alcoholics have led to what can only be described as a broad-based social movement, involving educators, physicians, the juvenile justice system, and other workers who for years had been baffled by what seemed to be inexplicable behavior in children and adults alike, behavior that has turned out to be closely linked to the experience of being raised as a child in an alcoholic family.

Always I have known at a very deep level that God loves me, and I have learned that my family loved me the best they knew how. I have learned to ask for help when I need it. I have also learned **to love unconditionally**, and that feels wonderful.

Recently, my Higher Power brought me to a path where I met a soulmate, my husband Joe. In a very profound way, I have found a "homecoming." (Later in the book, I will explain homecoming in more detail.) It is wonderful to rest, to be quiet, to feel a close bond with a person, a kindred soul, where honesty and intimacy can flourish in an atmosphere that encourages continued exploration and growth.

Perhaps this quiet Inner Peace is what I've been searching for since I was a little girl, looking for a way to feel safe, looking for a place to be safe. I have found what I sought, the way, the place, and the safety.

And I bring the message to others — to co-dependents and children of alcoholics of all ages: Full recovery does happen. It is not easy. It does not happen by itself.

Risk, change, belief in a Higher Power, and an outstretched hand to other people — all these can indeed lead to a sense of comfort, safety, warmth, love, and fulfillment.

I know. I have traveled the road. And it's been worth every mile of the journey, one day at a time.

4

Adult Children of Alcoholics (And Their Parents)

When does a child become an adult? At eighteen? At twenty-one? There is no exact age, no chronologically-fixed instant in time, that marks the youth's passage into adulthood. Adulthood is a social and legal convention. We have all known, at one time or another, an "adult" who acted childish, who displayed childish mannerisms, who seemed shallow and immature — an adult, in short, who didn't "act his or her age." And we have also seen children who seemed mature beyond their years, biologically immature adults who disdained the whippersnapper's spontaneity and mischievous delight in romp and uproar.

And then there's the "Adult Child." Where does the term "Adult Child" come from? And what are the implications for someone who has adult child characteristics?

Dr. Harry Tiebout once characterized the alcoholic as "King Baby." Recently, Dr. Joseph R. Cruse saw a parallel to the alcoholic King Baby in the origins of the "Adult Child King Baby."

More King Babies
Adult Children of Alcoholics

Families are the nucleus of our society . . .
Children are the nucleus of the family . . .
And they know it!
They start out as "King Baby."
They rule their world.

They do not question their power — it's there from
the beginning.
They confirm their power repeatedly every day.
They are center stage in the morning.
They are center stage all day.
They are certainly center stage at bedtime.

They have little doubt that this man and this
woman exist and are together for the sole purpose
of raising them.

With this in mind, little wonder (but adults are
surprised to find out) that they take full respon-
sibility and blame for all the trouble that may
beset the family.

They don't question it or voice it, and we don't
know to inform them of their error, which is
carried by them through life . . .

In an earlier chapter, I referred to Jael Greenleaf's term, "Para-alcoholic." Greenleaf states that the child from the alcoholic family is a para-alcoholic, influenced by both parents in the family, the addicted parent as well as the co-dependent or co-alcoholic spouse.

The child, both psychologically and situationally helpless, **is** trapped in the alcoholic family. On the other hand, the adult co-alcoholic **feels** trapped and psychologically helpless.

I believe that when the child moves to an adult situationally, when the youth becomes biologically mature and moves into socially conventional adulthood, the person takes on the "adult child" form of co-dependency. While the child matures physically, socially and chronologically, the inside emotional self remains underdeveloped, like a butterfly forever caught in the chrysalis stage, stuck and unfulfilled.

Janet Woititz has compiled a list of broad generalizations that she has gleaned from meetings with groups of adult children of alcoholics. Woititz says these traits emerge virtually every time adult children of alcoholics get together and discuss their experiences in growing up in alcoholic families.

Says Woititz:

Adult children of alcoholics . . .

. . . guess at what normal behavior is.

. . . have difficulty following a project through from beginning to end.

. . . lie when it would be just as easy to tell the truth.

. . . judge themselves without mercy.

. . . have difficulty having fun.

. . . take themselves very seriously.

. . . have difficulty with intimate relationships.

. . . over-react to changes over which they have no control.

. . . constantly seek approval and affirmation.

. . . usually feel that they are different from other people.

. . . are super-responsible or super-irresponsible.

. . . are extremely loyal even in the face of evidence that the loyalty is undeserved.

. . . are impulsive. They tend to lock themselves into a course of action without giving serious consideration to alternative behaviors or possible consequences.

This impulsivity leads to confusion, self-loathing and loss of control over their environment. In addition, they spend an excessive amount of energy cleaning up the mess.

In the words of Dr. Tim Cermak, adult children are "hypervigilant." They learned to watch, listen and protect themselves during their childhood. A central part of this early learning was geared toward self-protection, self-preservation. Adult children learned to scan the scene for signs of impending trouble.

And adult children tend to be proud of their control — holding in anger, compassion, love, and tears. Adult children deny vulnerability. As a result, they pay big prices in stress-related illnesses and lack of intimacy in relationships.

Adult children often keep up many myths about the family system and their life history. They build myths and fantasies to fill in missing pieces of childhood. They tenaciously hang on to denial:

"Our family always loved holidays and we had super times together."

"My mom and dad hardly ever argued or fought with each other."

"My grandparents didn't have any problems with drinking."

Facing the past honestly generates feelings of betrayal in adult children. They prefer to hold on to the myths.

Well, why not? What's wrong with clinging to myths? What's the harm? And more: What's to be gained by going back to the past and poking around and reviving unpleasant memories?

What happened in our alcoholic families influenced our behavior as children, and we have carried a portion of the past into our present lives. We may or may not be aware of the full impact of the past on our present, but it is usually well worth the effort to explore the connection.

A heritage of fear and mistrust undermines our growth. Discernment and careful choicemaking are assets and work to our advantage, work to enable us to fulfill our unique potentials. Thus, to begin recovery, adult children must relinquish the illusions about their families. They must face the facts about their parents and allow themselves to grieve the myth.

It is important for adult chidren to explore the emotional deprivation they experienced growing up in an alcoholic family and to grieve the loss of childhood. Only then can true memories emerge, only then can accurate feelings, long trapped and submerged, bubble to the surface. Healing can happen only in the presence of truth.

Many adult children have a lifetime of stored disappointments, hurt feelings, broken promises, and lonely, empty hours. And there is a pent-up rage they feel, a fulminating, all-consuming anger that's been bottled up for many years. At some time there will be a crack in the facade, and anger will explode outwardly, potently, explosively. Or it will implode, turn into depression, despondency, or even suicide. Or it will express itself in physical illness.

Intervention With The Adult Child

Growing up in alcoholic families, adult children developed communication styles that
    . . . impede honest sharing
    . . . prevent emotional intimacy
    . . . restrict healthy expression of feelings
    . . . foster dependency and reduce self-worth
    . . . avoid necessary conflict and produce tension

. . . neglect fun and pleasure

It is important that some kind of intervention take place that will aid an adult child to seek professional therapy, or to become part of a support group where impaired communication styles can undergo change.

There are three forms of "natural intervention" that can take place in the absence of other kinds of interventions: Crisis (career dissatisfaction, relocation, divorce, addiction). Stress-related illness (migraine, ulcers, colitis, anorexia). Death (through neglect, denial of life-threatening symptomatology, impulsive risk-taking, or suicide).

Fortunately, we do not have to wait for a natural intervention to take place. There are growing numbers of educational materials and other resources — books, pamphlets and articles — about the adult child. Support groups have sprung up across the country — Al-Anon support groups for adult children of alcoholics, as well as ACoA groups (or sometimes called ACA groups), that function as self-help groups for adult children in much the same way as AA works for alcoholics and Al-Anon for spouses. Two excellent sources of information are:

Al-Anon . . . Check the Yellow Pages, or get in touch through AA or Intergroup

National Association for Children of Alcoholics (NACoA), 31706 Coast Highway, Suite 201, South Laguna, CA 92677.

Clearly, the kind of intervention that takes place most often with ACoAs is more like a form of self-intervention. "Structured intervention" seldom occurs — for one reason, the adult child "passes," melds into the rest of society, works, has a family, diligently fulfills responsibilities — not like the alcoholic whose life is destroyed by a specific substance.

In other words, the adult child is virtually indistinguishable from other responsible adults in society, so it is hard to get "data," hard to get friends or relatives to agree to a confrontation, hard to have consequences if the adult child refuses treatment.

Intervention with the adult child is not so much intervention in the sense of pressure from others, as it is an attraction to a more comfortable way of life, an attraction to less stress, more self-awareness, and less emotional turbulence. It's an attraction to intimacy and to the end of loneliness.

The most common intervention comes from word of mouth, literature, and training seminars. As I have noted previously, many adult children are attracted to the helping professions. Now we are finding that the adult children among them are the first to go for training sessions. These professionals then take their new-found information back to their peers and clients, and the movement spreads and grows.

But even though the adult child has much to gain, there is, as we have seen, much pain to go through. Bob Subby, an adult child who is also a very dear friend, summed up what the adult child faces in finishing unfinished business on the journey to self-knowledge:

> Compensators, controllers, manipulators, avoiders, deniers . . . all these and more are the many descriptive words used to identify us. We are emotionally and socially immature. We operate out of a framework filled with free-floating anxiety as a result of accumulated layers of unfinished business in our family history. We are most often motivated by guilt and shame, always seeking to relieve the stress of these emotional phantoms. We are spiritually divided from ourselves, and so are unable to reveal to others what we can no longer see. Intimacy is a goal; but as individuals not familiar or intimate with ourselves, we are unable to develop real closeness with others. Lost, defiant, confused, pessimistic, mistrusting, angry and

afraid, we have become defensive and seek only from those who are like us.

Black and white are the attitudes we hide behind to avoid the stress that always precedes change. Crying for help in a language that few understand, wishing to be heard but denying the confrontations of truth — liars who have the truth, but believe as the wounded child in our history that we will, as before, be hurt in our sharing. Running, always running, creating the crisis, only to divert our pressures, and we rest only in the clouds of confusion. We have survived by our wits and our will. We must not be broken, but shaped by the constancy of love that holds firmly to those values which promote life, model wholeness, and give hope. Only those things will we hear, for the child in us believes as a victim and sees no choice or avenue of escape . . .

— From one who survived with love

The point is: Bob **did** recover. Bob survived with love. Bob faced the unpleasant reality of history and confirmed the fact that only in accurate assessment of reality can healing take place. There was, to be sure, pain to be endured as Bob took apart the myths of childhood — myths that were like unhealed scabs on festering wounds. But once exposed to care, to the healing power of illumination and love, the wounds healed.

How can the adult child set about to finish unfinished business?

1. First of all, find out as much as you can about the actual happenings in your family of origin. What really took place? When? Who else was there? Face it, corroborate it, feel it, and be honest with yourself.

2. Allow all the feelings to surface. Talk about those feelings in a safe environment, with other adult children in a group, or with a therapist — with someone who knows about alcoholism, and who has a grasp of family dynamics.

3. Start making behavior changes yourself. Take the initiative. Be satisfied with small changes, working up to whatever change, large or small, that will improve the quality of your life.

4. Put yourself in an environment where you can experience deep emotional healing. This might be in a treatment program, a specific workshop designed for adult children, a spiritual setting, or a weekend retreat. The important thing to remember is to be with others who know the healing process, who understand adult child issues and problems, and who have a grasp of family dynamics.

We'll explore this process more fully in Part Two of this book.

The Child Within

The notion of the "child within" has been one of the most helpful concepts for adult children of alcoholics. We have seen how children of alcoholics have been encouraged to grow up fast, to become small versions of adulthood. And at the same time they remain emotionally vulnerable, and their child of joy and vision and feeling was tucked away inside. In cold storage. Warehoused.

The time has come, now that we understand this phenomenon, to go back inside and retrieve the lost little child who has been waiting to grow up and have its proper place in our lives. At the time of our birth, our inside self and our outside **self** are equal. Who we appear to be on the outside is who we are on the inside. As we learn to deny who we are, and as we try too hard to live up to others' expectations, our real self gets stuck and our public self gets distorted. To change this co-dependent pattern of living, we need to make friends with, and nurture the child within us we left behind.

I would like to suggest a simple exercise. Find a quiet place to sit down and have a talk with your inner child. An honest, unself-conscious talk. Let yourself go quietly into your heart and recognize that small child who became silent, who became guarded, who retreated behind cunningly crafted barriers.

Give your little child within permission to come out into the light today, to enter the world and see it whole. Let your little child within know that it's safe

   . . . to grow up

. . . to accept love
. . . to share personal feelings when appropriate
. . . to spend some time each day in pleasure and play.

Tell your inner child that it's okay to decide who you want to spend time with, and who you'd rather not pal around with. It's okay to decide what to accept from others and what to reject.

Tell your inner child that it's expected to be honest, that it's expected to begin making major decisions in its own behalf.

Talk to the child within, and the child within will respond. The child within understands. The inner child knows . . . Ben Whitney gives us a glimpse of the inner child in his poem, "The Child Knows."

THE CHILD KNOWS

Our truth
once known
waits, ever present.
Never lost, only obscured or ignored
never separate, only divided from us, by us.
Not to be seen, thought, studied, or explained
neither captured, created nor held
not a gift
but divine birthright.
Our truth
undiminished
perpetual in its patience
waits for the discovery.
Silently waiting
for us to return, to rejoin
to know what was always there.

Ask, the child knows.

5

Parenting The Adult Child

ACoA Recovery: The Parents' Role

What happens when, after many years of silence, observing the no-talk rule and avoiding conflict, family members begin to talk to each other? Sundering the silence — breaking the no-talk rule — produces many new feelings.

Many recovering alcoholic parents suffer over the years from "recovery guilt" — a burdensome, inescapable feeling that "their" illness had adversely affected the spouse and children. However, new knowledge about the depth and significance of the co-dependency illness can help the alcoholic put long-felt guilt into perspective. Recovering parents might even begin to realize that much of their recovery guilt is really anger — anger at feeling solely responsible for what happened in the family system.

And what about the adult child? It's important to understand that many of the symptoms exhibited by adult children have been highly approved by our society. Only recently have we been able to identify the pain behind the behavior. Only recently have adult children felt safe enough to begin talking about how they really feel.

There's another factor to take into consideration: The transgenerational nature of the adult child syndrome. Many parents of adult children overlook the fact that they too are adult children from their own families of origin. In other words, the parents themselves had parents who were alcoholics. It's a vicious cycle of addiction and co-dependency, repeated again and again.

Should we try at this point to untangle the strands of influence to determine exactly who did what to whom? And where, and when? Those are Herculean tasks — pursuits that could easily divert us from more important issues.

Instead, we should encourage each person to take responsibility for himself at this time in life. We should encourage each adult child and each parent to begin to share freely their feelings and needs with loved ones. And they should openly discuss and actively explore ways to set limits with each other, while at the same time giving each other support in moving toward full recovery.

Guilt and Avoidance

Within the framework of guilt, a subtle form of avoidance permeates parent/child relationships. The avoidance has a cyclical quality. A few of these repetitious and fairly predictable parent/child transactions include:

- Rehashing . . . talking over and over the same issues, the same arguments, with never any permanent, mutually-satisfactory resolution.
- Blaming . . . wanting the other person to change before one can feel better — fault-finding as a strategy of motivating the other person to change, a strategy that generally turns out to be futile.
- Playing Scapegoat . . . assuming the guilt mantle, readily acquiescing, taking all the blame as a means of inducing guilt in others and controlling their behavior.

- Playing D.A. . . . continually prying into each other's affairs, snooping and expressing suspicion about each other's motives, honesty, rectitude, and so on.
- Judging . . . watching, carefully scrutinizing, every activity — and being judgmental about each other, behaving like a self-righteous supervisor.
- Care-taking . . . being preoccupied with the welfare of others to the point of neglecting one's own feelings and issues.

Back and forth, the parent and adult child go . . . back and forth. It's like a game of ping-pong. Everyone is very busy, and there is constant action and something to do. Yet no one goes anywhere — except back . . . and . . . forth. Fundamentally, it turns out to be simply a way to keep busy and **appear** to be involved with each other. Ping-pong.

Yet the relationship is so tight that if a third person tries to intervene — offers suggestions or somehow poses a threat to interfere — the parent and adult child team up and join forces against the outsider, the intruder who would upset the precarious harmony. Although the parent and child ostensibly want each other to change, the prospect of actual change mediated by a third party is unacceptable.

At times, this parent/child bond is stronger and more intimate than the bond between both parents. In a painful marital situation, the parents often fail in setting appropriate boundaries in relationship to their children. Children may be invited, and even coerced, into closer sharing with a parent — a closer sharing that is unhealthy for both the parent and the child. In extreme forms, pressure for close sharing can be a kind of emotional incest. The close emotional ties sought by parents in such situations compensates for lack of emotional ties between mates.

The adult child may have a hard time accepting a parent's peers, friends, associates, and lovers. Similarly, the parent criticizes the adult child's choice of relationships, vocation, religion, and so on.

Symptoms	Society's View	Parents' Perception	Pathology	Child's Feelings
Workaholism	Successful Amer. Dream	Proud Success	Driven	Lonely/tired
Caretaker	Loving & Dependable	Mature & Responsible	Unable to get needs met	Unloved & inadequate
Controlling	Strong leaders	Organized	Manipulator	Afraid & unsure
Chronic, sickly	Fragile	Helpless	Manipulator	Angry
Anorexic	Fashionable	Attractive	Starving feelings	Inadequate & angry
Overweight	Scorned	Medical problem, "embarrassed"	Feeding feelings	Inadequate & angry
Perfectionistic	"Very" dependable	Wonderfully self-disciplined	Compulsive	Guilty & Inadequate
Relationship problems	Independent	Very selective High Standards	Inability to relate	Afraid/hurt
Peer worship	Conforming/cool	Friendly	Socially inept	Fear
Spouse surrogate	Close family relationship	"Daddy's Girl" "Mommy's Boy"	Emotional incest	Power
Emotional binging	Overly sensitive	Fully honest	Blaming/controlling	Righteousness
Undying loyalty	Brave, admirable	Traditional	Fear	Insecurity

Dr. Joe Cruse has put together a chart showing the differences between the social perception and the parental perception of the adult child's behavior, and contrasting those perceptions with what's really going on in the adult child.

Suggestions for Parents of Adult Children

It almost becomes a routine, a litany, this listing of woes and foibles — this recitation of the battles, the wounds, and the scars. And there comes a time when a recovering parent wants to cry, **"Enough!** Tell me what I can do to help— how do we break the cycle, how can I help my adult child recover?"

I have a few suggestions for parents who want to help their children recover from the family dynamics of alcoholism and co-dependency.

1. Most important, get help for yourself. Children have a need to see their parents as well and happy as possible. Take good care of yourself, and in doing so, you will become a role model, showing that it's desirable and quite all right to take care of yourself.

2. Be flexible regarding the demands you make on your children. Give them as much freedom and independence as possible. Do not make them feel as though their presence is the only thing that fulfills you. Find alternative plans for holidays and other former family traditions.

3. Let them know you love and respect who they are. Encourage them to seek information and try alternative choices until they find their own comfort level, their own satisfaction in career, relationships, and lifestyles.

4. Respect their maturity and demand that they also encourage you in your attempt to seek information and try alternative choices until you find your own level of comfort in career, relationships, and lifestyles.

5. Share your honest self with your children. At appropriate times, share your emotions (anger, hurt, excitement, fears, compassion, love), and also your thoughts and attitudes. Show them, rather than tell them, that emotional honesty

can build intimacy. Here is a perfect instance of the enduring wisdom that actions speak louder than words.

It will be easier and far more realistic for you to help your adult children if you feel good about yourself. Your children need two physically and emotionally whole adult parents — parents who may or may not have chosen to remain married. Your day-to-day responsibility for your children ended when your children left home. Your legal responsibility ended for them when they came of age.

Now your parenting role shifts into letting the children become fully functioning adults. And you continue to have an impact as a role model.

Dr. Joe Cruse has developed a short set of guidelines for the recovering parents of recovering adult children:

• Parents must accept that tradition does not rule family relationships with adult children. Parents and adult children alike can make choices, without guilt, about how to spend holidays, about information boundaries, about coupleship and so on. And without guilt. Just because it used to be done in a certain way does not mean it always must be done that way.

• Parents need to take their own freedom, and in doing so give freedom to their children.

• Parents can not only turn the relationships over to a Higher Power, they can also call the Higher Power in for help and turn to the task at hand. Take action!

• Parents need to insist on their parental birthright in the same way they give the children their birthrights.

    — Both have a right to dignity and respect.
    — Both have a right to say no.
    — Both have a right to stand up for self.
    — Both are entitled to truth and honesty in relationships.
    — Both have a right to change their mind.
    — Both have a right to a recovery program.

• Parents need to accept those things that cannot change — such as powerlessness over another person.

• Parents can stand ready to change self, but only in a manner acceptable to self, for the benefit of the relationship. (In other words, make no self-defeating sacrifices for the child.)

• Stand alert and communicative so that the wisdom to know the difference between what can be changed and what cannot be changed can be clearly and quickly put into action.

An important Big Lesson a parent needs to teach the adult child is:

> The adult child is a satellite, not the whole center of the parents' existence. The adult child has a separate life, and coupleship is by definition a twosome . . . and coupleship cannot involve a parent and child, for thereby it becomes emotionally incestuous.

> The adult child must come to know that the parents' coupleship and singleship are, to put it bluntly, "None of the adult child's business."

> And the parents, as grandparents, will know their message got across when they hear their child tell their adult kids,

> "We love you ... and we are none of your business."

Finally, as recovering parents of recovering adult children, be gentle with yourselves. In all my work with thousands of alcoholic family members over the years, I have never met one who deliberately set out to hurt a child in any way. Yet millions of children over time have been hurt — inadvertently, perhaps, unintentionally — but hurt all the same. Hurt physically and emotionally.

Many of those children are now themselves recovering parents. It is time we recognize that both alcoholism and co-dependency are aspects of the same hurtful disease process. We cannot change what happened during the time of pathology. And we cannot blame, for it was a time of contribution by all. We can only take responsibility for what we know and for what develops during recovery.

All of us, in our own way, may have amends to make. Make them once, and move on. Do not dwell on self-recrimination, do not brood on what might have been. Forgiveness of self and others is the beginning of healing for self and others. For everyone's sake, put more energy into forgiveness and healing.

My own work in developing the roles played by young children in dysfunctional families came from many hours of sitting in sessions with groups of children of alcoholics. The different behaviors I observed were really variations on the three components of co-dependency: Emotional, social and physical dependency.

Young children's reality was the predictable pattern of addiction and co-dependency in the home. Family stress, chaos, and upset became the norm for these children. It is no wonder, then, that as adult children they rely on **denial** to maintain the status quo. And no wonder they continue to deny the possibility of change for the better, when childhood ideas, observations, and behaviors were "normally" painful. The roles children fall back on — Hero, Scapegoat, Lost Child, and Mascot — are unaware, desperate attempts to cover up painful feelings.

All the components of adult co-dependency are normal and regular components of childhood in a painful family. Full-blown co-dependency and addiction are very predictable outcomes for children of alcoholics. I truly believe that treatment of today's children from alcoholic and other painful homes will be the best prevention of another generation of chemically dependent persons.

Part Two: Freedom To

What does **Freedom To** mean? What does it mean to be "free to" as opposed to being "free from?"

Freedom To involves the first step following surrender to the presence of the disease — chemical dependency or co-dependency. At the moment of surrender, one experiences a "freedom from," a letting go, an unburdening.

The next important step comes when the person thoughtfully asks, "Now what?" **Freedom To** is the "Now . . . **This!**"

Freedom To is all about learning:

Choicemaking
New Information
Risking
Trying out new behaviors

Freedom To means taking action toward whatever will bring about healing and a new, fulfilling lifestyle.

Traditionally, family treatment has been the arena in which people learned they had choices — and learned to find new choices. However, too many treatment programs stopped with awareness and education. Too few pursued **Freedom To** through the steps of confrontation, risk and accountability. **Freedom To** means behavior change and action in new arenas.

6

Family Therapy and Individual Recovery

Over the past few years, alcoholism and other drug dependencies have slowly entered the mainstream health care delivery system. The word is out: Alcoholics and other addicts can overcome chemical dependency. **Alcoholics can and do recover.**

But the role of family members in the addiction process remains enshrouded in obscurity, poorly understood and neglected both by professionals in the addictions field, and by the public at large.

Is it true that the family is relatively unimportant in recovery? Can the addicted person recover and re-enter the family and life go on as usual?

In the 1930s and 1940s, when treatment for the addictions was rare, if not unknown, Alcoholics Anonymous performed an invaluable service by helping alcoholics get well through abstinence, fellowship, and spiritual discovery. Seeing the success of Alcoholics Anonymous, Lois W. recognized the special needs of family members, and was instrumental in founding Al-Anon in 1951. In the Al-Anon pamphlet, "Lois's Story," Lois W. described the growth of Al-Anon:

> *Soon, small groups, composed of the families of AA members sprang up all over the country. They had a three-fold purpose: to grow spiritually through living by the Twelve Steps of Alcoholics Anonymous; to give encouragement and understanding to the alcoholic in the home; and to welcome and give comfort to the families of new or prospective AA members.*

Together, A.A. and Al-Anon constituted a foundation and a framework that took into account the needs of other members of the family, as well as the addicted person. Later, under the auspices of Al-Anon, the first Alateen group was formed to deal specifically with issues central to younger relatives and friends of alcoholics. The teengers themselves conduct the meetings, with guidance from an Al-Anon member.

When professionals began to design formalized, structured treatment regimens for alcoholics and other addicts, most programs keyed on the alcoholic, on the addicted person. If the family members were considered at all, they were cast in the role of **villains:** What was the spouse doing that was driving the alcoholic to drink? How were the family members putting intolerable pressure on the chemically addicted person?

In the late 1960s, research began to show that family members themselves were affected by the addiction process in the family. Margaret Cork, a Canadian researcher, interviewed children from alcoholic homes and published the results of her book in *The Forgotten Children* (1969). However, the time was not ripe for widespread recognition of the trauma of growing up in an alcoholic home, and Cork's pioneering work remained virtually forgotten until the 1980s.

Al-Anon and Alateen were the major support groups for family members, but formal treatment for the family took a long time to evolve. The early family programs were mainly education. "This is what alcoholism is all about," the family was instructed. "Alcoholism is a disease, and this is how it works, and here are a few ways the family can help the alcoholic get well and stay well." The focus continued to be on the alcoholic, and family members were urged to be accepting and to be understanding about the addict's special needs during the recovery process.

These early programs, limited and superficial, were well-received in some areas of the country. Alcohol education for the family did not illuminate the darkness, but it sparked interest and fueled a small flame of hope for the family. After all, family members, isolated and confused, felt grateful for all the information and sense of participation they could get.

In other areas of the country, family education fell flat. Unenthusiastic professionals placed small emphasis on family involvement of any kind. Family education programs were poorly attended, discounted, disparaged and minimized.

By the 1970s, "Family Week" had begun to appear in the standard 28-day alcoholism treatment program. However, the concept of Family Week was not well-standardized. In some programs, it was education — information disseminated by a lecturer, using films and discussion groups. But increasingly, Family Week took the form of education plus therapy. The educational component was seen to be important because family members needed accurate information about the disease of alcoholism. Therapy came to be seen as equally important — important as a means of letting family members learn about themselves, learn to see their role in the alcoholic's addiction.

Through therapy, the family began to see how alcoholism afflicted **the whole family** — alcoholic, spouse and children. The family began to see that they were **affected** by an illness, true. But they also began to recognize a more fundamental process at work: The family began to realize that alcoholism is a **family illness.**

Even though the notion of alcoholism as a family illness took hold in many places during the 1970s, there was still a great deal of confusion about family treatment in various treatment centers. For example, some treatment programs didn't add a Family Week, they patched on something called a "family program." It could mean two nights a week, Or a Sunday afternoon. It could mean a family counseling session.

Or it could mean a session of watching various films about alcoholism. There were many films on "family illness." A film called "The Summer We Moved To Elm Street," for example, was a poignant portrait of alcoholism in the family, seen through the eyes of a little girl. "Elm Street" showed family alcoholism, but without resolution, without a sense that there was some way to interrupt the pattern of family destruction that was taking place. Films can be an excellent way of raising awareness about alcoholism, but too often they were of little practical value for the family.

To be fair, the lack of emphasis on family very likely resulted from the type of patient who entered treatment. The typical alcoholic in treatment tended to be an unemployed male, single, separated or divorced. And the alcoholic came to treatment in the late stages of the disease, generally after all resources were exhausted and the family had fallen apart. [For years, women alcoholics remained closeted with the disease "hidden" and untreated. Men divorced their alcoholic wives much more readily than wives divorced their alcoholic husbands.]

However, as alcoholics came to be identified at earlier stages — through DWI programs, Family Intervention Programs, and Employee Assistance Programs — they entered treatment with families intact and jobs to go back to. That's when pressure began to build for increased family involvement.

Unfortunately, as we have seen, efforts to involve families have been unclear and inconsistent. Family treatment is a complex area. Counselor training programs traditionally focus on the alcoholic, not the family. Professionals have evolved a variety of theories and philosophies of treatment. Conflicting philosophies spawn diverse programs, making it difficult for families — and other professionals — to decide what course to take, what kind of help to seek. In addition, insurance carriers have been slow to recognize the importance of family treatment, making it a costly add-on to the "standard" treatment regimen.

Alcoholism Treatment In A Nutshell

For purposes of clarity, I would briefly like to define some commonly-used terms, and then I would like to suggest **what** is needed to treat adequately the kindred illnesses of chemical dependency and co-dependency.

Alcoholism Treatment: A generic term covering a variety of individual and group counseling efforts, usually, and most productively, aimed at breaking patterns of drinking and bolstering the paramount importance of abstinence from alcohol and other addicting chemicals. Inpatient programs may vary from 10 days to 28 days in length. Depending on the level of treatment (or severity of diagnosis), outpatient programs may vary from daily meetings over an eight-week period, to structured group programs meeting from one to three times per week over a twelve-week period. Some inpatient programs include a weekly "aftercare" program for six to twelve months following inpatient treatment.

Focus of treatment is primarily on the alcoholic, not on spouses or other family members, although they may attend educational sessions to become more informed about the disease of alcoholism, to enable them to understand more fully what the alcoholic must deal with in recovery.

Treatment programs generally encourage the alcoholic to become involved with a support group, such as Alcoholics Anonymous. And spouses are encouraged to join Al-Anon.

Again, it must be stressed that there is a tremendous variety in treatment for alcoholism from state-to-state — and even within the same state. Alcoholism treatment does not come in a standard package, like aspirin. No FDA regulations govern the ingredients of alcoholism treatment. And alcoholism counselors and other treatment professionals do not go through standard training that insures that each comes out with a specified way of dealing with chemical dependency.

Co-dependency Treatment: One, two, three or four weeks of inpatient treatment focused on the illness of co-dependency. Or an outpatient structure over a varied time-frame, also aimed at the illness of co-dependency. Both inpatient and outpatient programs are designed to provide education, therapy groups and individually-designed treatment to confront the specialized issues of spouses, adult children of alcoholics and concerned person co-dependents. I'll go into co-dependency treatment in more detail a little later on in this section.

Family Education Program: May be short-term residential (three to five days), or outpatient involvement over a varied time frame. Education includes, as we have seen, films and lectures about alcoholism and about the effects of alcoholism on the family members.

Many programs also have small support groups where family members can meet together and share experiences and feelings about the impact of alcoholism on each of them and about problems arising during the recovery process. Sometimes there are individual family sessions with a counselor.

I firmly believe that those who offer family education programs and family members who attend family education should view the process in its rightful perspective — as **education** — and that following education, family members should be referred to family therapy or co-dependency treatment.

Family Therapy: A time to bring "treated" individuals together to examine family relationships and dynamics, and to re-negotiate communication among these "treated" individuals.

Almost inevitably, one of the family members — usually the alcoholic, and less often the spouse — has received some form of structured treatment, while other family members have received education only (and in some places, not even education). **Family therapy with partially or inconsistently treated family members is, in my experience, extremely difficult and somewhat superficial. Unfortunately, it also has few lasting effects.**

To make family therapy have a more thorough and lasting effect, professionals need to discard out-dated terminology, to discard antiquated conceptual models, and to transcend obsolete training. **Up-to-date therapy models and fresh attitudes are necessary as we learn more about the full illness of chemical dependency and co-dependency.**

Now let's take a closer look at Co-dependency Treatment and Family Therapy, followed by a special section of Family Reconstruction.

Once treatment addresses each of these symptom areas for each one of the co-dependents, then families will have the tools to negotiate relationships from a position of freedom and strength rather than to let the relationships take place passively, by default.

Family therapy, with couples or with full family sessions, is not merely possible, not merely feasible, it is essential. Increasingly among professionals working in the field of chemical dependency, family therapy has gained recognition as an integral part of a treatment plan leading to full recovery — for the family as a whole, not just for one select member only.

Co-Dependency
Treatment

SYMPTOMS	GOAL OF TREATMENT
Denial and Self-Delusion	Recognition and acceptance of one's own defenses and dysfunctions — best accomplished in group therapy, with education.
Compulsive Behavior	Facing co-dependent compulsions (workaholism, obesity, smoking, sexual acting-out, clinging, passivity, etc . . .) and starting a program of recovery. Best accomplished through a combination of education and structured group therapy.
Repressed Feelings	Experiential therapy will make possible experiential expression of feelings, which is essential to healing. Both self-help groups and highly-skilled therapy groups are necessary to make this healing possible. Feelings must be expressed and re-experienced for healing to take place.
Low Self Worth	Working the 12-Step Program, expressing resentments, and going through the grief process make it possible to learn self-forgiveness and self-acceptance.
Medical Complications	Medical problems should be addressed immediately. Stress-related chronic symptoms will begin to clear up as soon as a person begins to work a consistent, well-structured healing program.

Family Therapy

In family therapy, two or more members of a family come together to work out problems that exist in relationships. The problems may exist in any combination of relationships. The coupleship relationship needs much work, as two people negotiate new ways of being — including a more intimate and vulnerable sharing. There are often generational hurts and resentments between siblings and parents.

Thorny problems between a parent and an adult child may emerge — especially when the adult child has been acting like a spouse during the time of illness, and wants to continue playing an interfering role as the parents try to heal their coupleship.

One of my most difficult cases was a 28-year-old girl who simply didn't want to allow her divorced father the privacy or emotional freedom to develop a new love relationship. She had been his support and enabler during his drinking years, and she wanted to remain his best friend in recovery.

In cases where there are "other" relationships, such as cooks, maids, secretaries, bodyguards, managers, and family lawyers, they, too, may be included in some of the family sessions. In short, a family session may include anyone who has a close relationship with any member of the family.

Families that find themselves torn apart by stress and conflict have generally operated for years with a set of spoken and unspoken rules, verbal and non-verbal communications — rules and messages that set impossible standards and create an atmosphere in which low self-worth flourishes.

Impossible standards — rigorous family rules — go against the humanness of family members. Predictably, unworkable rules insure failure and a sense of inadequacy. And they produce guilt and shame abundantly.

Here's a list of some of the unworkable rules found in dysfunctional families:

- Boys shouldn't cry. (They should be like diminutive adult males, independent, self-contained and tough. They should bear pain and hurt with a kind of stoicism and emotional flatness exemplified by rugged males in cigarette commercials and by romantic depictions of fighters in the wild, wild West.)
- Girls should always be nice. (Talk nice talk. Never say anything negative. Do nice things. Never do anything that would make someone look askance at you. Nice girls . . . **Don't.**)
- Elders always deserve respect and come first. (No matter how the elder behaves, the elder must be treated gingerly, for an elder has power — even if it's used capriciously and irrationally.)
- There is only one way to do things. (That is, there's one **right** way to do things. There's only one right way to deal with a spouse, to handle the kids, to have a birthday party, to dance . . .)
- Don't talk, think or feel about sex, money and feelings. (Talk . . . well, talk stirs things up, gets people upset, and when people get upset, well, it just causes more trouble. When it comes to sex, money and feelings, silence takes on a precious eloquence. Silence is not only golden, it's high-grade platinum.)
- Work first, play later. (Much later . . .)
- The older child must always set an example for the younger children. (A good example, that is.)
- Children should always obey their parents. (And it's the parents' job to see that their children make the **right** decisions — the decisions the parents want. Then when the child reaches the magic age of emancipation — 18 or 21 — the Good Decision Fairy will plink the child on the skull with a charmed wand and make the child a full-fledged Adult who always makes Good Decisions.

- Don't talk about your family to anyone outside the family. (Outsiders will just spread malicious gossip. So always pretend that everything's okay at home, even if it isn't. There's nothing worse than being disloyal to your family.)

The list could go on and on. To some degree, all of us get programmed to live by one or more of these expectations. But in dysfunctional families, in families torn by conflict and strife, these rules and expectations color most of the family relationships. When family members try to live up to unworkable rules, the inevitable result is failure. And anger. And inadequacy and guilt.

There is a way out, however. These impossible rules and expectations aren't chiseled in granite on the high wind-swept slopes of some imperishable mountaintop. The unworkable rules reside inside our heads, and we can change them.

To counteract old, unworkable family expectations, we can learn to give ourselves new messages of self-worth. We can affirm ourselves. We can reprogram our out-dated thinking with affirmations, with messages that reassure us, that promote our self-worth. And as we do, as we practice affirmations and begin to look at ourselves in a new way, we will discover that others will begin to respond to our strengths. Others will treat us differently, and they, too, will begin to affirm us.

The following are examples of affirmations:
- I'm a good person. (Instead of "I'm a bad person.")
- I've tried to do the best I could under some pretty tough circumstances. (Instead of "I never do anything right.")
- I am a smart person. (Instead of "I'm so dumb.")
- It's okay to want people to like me. (Instead of "It's a sign of weakness to be liked by others.")
- I am lovable. (Instead of "I am unlovable.")
- It's all right to express anger. (Instead of "It's bad to feel or to express anger.")

- It's normal to have fears. (Instead of "Only crazy or weak people have fears, and I have fears, therefore ...")
- It's a sign of courage to risk, even when failure follows. (Instead of "It's better to be safe and never try, than to take a chance and fail.")
- It's normal to be jealous from time to time. (Instead of "I should never feel jealous under any circumstances.")
- It's okay not to like everyone. (Instead of "I should try my hardest to like everyone and if I don't, I'm a bad person.")

. . . These examples could be multiplied many times over. The essential thing to keep in mind is the **affirmation**, the iteration and reiteration of self-worth.

Those who work with families soon find out that the survival strength developed by children and adults in painful families can become a handicap to a recovering adult. **Our strength has often kept us so tightly under control that we have been invulnerable to the love and care that might have come our way.**

There's value in knowing that we have an inner reservoir of strength that helps us survive tough situations. But unless we allow our defenses to relax, we may end up lonely and alone.

In both family therapy and co-dependency treatment, I believe that it's necessary to use experiential tools in order to help people express their vulnerability in a safe setting. Thoughts, concepts, abstract learnings can be important, but they do not, by themselves, bring about deep and inner healing.

Following the healing process, education plays a very important role in helping people understand what happened, why it happened, and how life can be different with new attitudes and new behaviors. However, trying to teach a course on anatomy and bone structure to someone with a painful broken leg — before taking time to set the leg and make the injured person comfortable, is silly at best, cruel, inhumane and unethical at worst.

Trying to give new information to someone in emotional pain is no different. There will be time for information and abstract concepts after therapy — after the discharge of feelings. And the family members or co-dependents will be much more receptive to the new learning once emotional re-education has taken place.

Here is the context in which emotional re-education takes place. It is a context where . . .

Accumulated anger has brought about a great deal of "perceived depression." Accumulated guilt has brought about a great deal of "perceived shame." Accumulated avoidance has brought about a great deal of "perceived fear." Accumulated compulsive drives have brought about a great deal of "fatigue." Accumulated **denial** of these feelings has brought about a great deal of inadequacy.

The healing process must take place in an environment where each of the family members can feel safe to feel and to express rage, guilt, fear, inadequacy, shame, tiredness, grief, and so on. It's important to express feelings, to let the feelings actually take place and not to merely discuss them in an abstract fashion. Talking "about" feelings may seem to render them safe, may seem to neutralize them. But it's a phony kind of safety, characteristic of a kind of **intellectualized therapy** that talks about the problems, but **in the end leaves the problems** much the same as they were in the beginning — unchanged, unresolved.

One method to help co-dependents and families wake up repressed and denied feelings involves "reliving the experience" — and it has proved to be one of the most valuable tools I've ever used with families and co-dependents in treatment.

Family Restoration (Reconstruction)

Over the years, I have developed short-term programs (based on my work with Virginia Satir) for co-dependents and the professionals who work with them. I call these short-term programs "Family Restoration" or "Family Reconstruction." Family Restoration is not meant to be all-inclusive in its focus on the process of co-dependent treatment.

I view Family Restoration as a structured setting in which profound learnings and feelings take place — events that re-orient recovery paths. Family Restoration can be seen as a thinking-feeling intervention that paves the way for a more thorough recovery program. Let me explain . . .

Not long ago, I ran across a definition of experience as "history plus feelings." Perhaps the experience most common to every culture is that its children grow up in **families** — be they nuclear families, extended families, or communal in form. Obviously, this experience — the family — has a profound effect on the kind of adults we become. One of the themes of this book has been to explore some of the experiences of children who grow up in families touched by alcoholism.

In Chapter 3 — "My Story" — I have written at length of my own experience. My family "history" is full of episodes associated with my parents' alcoholism. The "feelings" I had were a confused mixture of guilt, shame and hurt when my parents were drinking. And I felt love, comfort and security when my parents were sober. At either emotional pole, I had to wonder if I weren't crazy to feel so pulled apart in my emotional life.

I responded by being super-responsible so that I could be a rallying point for my parents, younger brother and sister. I worked to be popular, became the star of the debate team and the apple of my father's eye. I succeeded, in short, in becoming the Family Princess. And my parents' drinking persisted.

The message: **Try harder!**

Small wonder, then, that the driving force of my adult life was to "try harder." And harder. And harder. And still, I could never be satisfied with anything I did. Life for me seemed an endless series of efforts that inevitably fell short: I was striving for an ideal that did not exist!

My own cycle of despair and confusion was broken several years ago by my "Reconstruction" with Virginia Satir, author of *Peoplemaking* and an early pathfinder in the field of family therapy. One day she guided me through a tableau of events from my family's past, lovingly re-enacted by her other students. With their support, I relived my childhood and felt once again the fear and confusion of seeing my parents fight at the dinner table, of seeing my father "asleep" on the floor, of feeling my mother's love and support for me drained under the pressures of the illness of alcoholism. I relived my teenage and adult years through re-creation of other vignettes culled from my memory.

"Going through this experience was one of the highlights of my life . . ."
— Virginia Satir

When the Reconstruction ended, I had relived a lifetime of pain. I had re-felt my feelings and discarded the ones which were no longer useful or appropriate. And I paused a moment to cherish the feelings that had given me pleasure.

I made many choices the day of my Reconstruction. And while I would stop short in saying that I was reborn a healthy Choicemaker in the space of that one day, I will say — unequivocally — that the experience turned my life around so that I could build from a healthy base. I took control of my life, rather than continue to be controlled by feelings triggered by the illness of co-dependency.

Today, one of the greatest joys of my life is guiding others through "Family Reconstruction" so that they too may leave old issues behind and become healthy Choicemakers.

Virginia Satir's "Reconstruction" of me was done in her own very special style, and I am indebted to her. In the intervening years, I have evolved my own style of Reconstruction, based upon additional knowledge derived from working with alcoholic families. In order to separate and make clear the differences between Satir's approach to Reconstruction and my own, I use the term "Family Restoration" for my work with families and co-dependents.

My Family Restoration workshops always begin on a Sunday evening. At the start, most of the participants are strangers to each other. Each person introduces himself to the group and may talk about his personal goals over the next four days. The evening of introduction is always special to me because I know that this group of strangers will know each other very well before the week is over.

Monday is a day of learning about alcoholism, drug abuse, family systems, and birth order. My professional life has been dedicated to changing our cultural and political views of alcoholism. It is not merely the disease of the dependent person (the afflicted one). As we have seen, alcoholism is a family disease, a primary illness affecting every member of the family.

I emphasize the fact that when chemical addiction occurs in one member of the family, the other members adapt to that person's unstable behavior by developing behavior of their own that causes the least amount of personal stress. These mutual accommodations and adaptations protect each person's feeling life, so the family survives — but the survival is a warped and deluded one.

Next I talk about the family roles that I saw emerge in my own clinical experience:

• **The Enabler** — Usually the spouse who does "everything under the sun" to make the drinking spouse stop, except what works: confronting the user or leaving the relationship.

• **The Family Hero** — Who sees and hears what is happening and takes responsibility for the family by becoming successful and popular.

• **The Family Scapegoat** — Who rejects the family system by running away, withdrawal, or defiant behavior.

• **The Lost Child** — Who quietly and unobtrusively withdraws from the family system.

• **The Mascot** — Who hides his pain with humor and provides the system with "comic relief."

I've explained these roles in more detail in my previous book, *Another Chance*. All these roles are symptoms of the disease of co-dependency, in which the primary compulsion is to act in a manner which accommodates the dependent. It is a primary, progressive and chronic disease that stands between the afflicted person and his ability to **act** from free choice rather than **react**, or to continue behaving in the way he learned in order to survive a sick situation.

On Monday, many people who were heretofore unfamiliar with my work, come to terms with their own knowledge and feelings about co-dependency. They see themselves for the first time as people who experienced a painful family system, as people who never left that family system emotionally. With their family issues suddenly "crystallized," they now have a look into their own behavior patterns and feelings, and something to work with over the next few days.

Tuesday morning, the psychodrama of "Reconstruction" (now "Restoration") begins. For the "Star" — the person whose life we will be re-creating all day and evening — the event began months before with his selection for that role. Once selected, the Star began amassing information about his family of origin, his grandparents' families, and the family in which he now lives. If he has done his job well, the Star will have a family tree, anecdotes and notable events securely in memory or on paper. He will have snapshots, portraits, birth certificates, court records, adoption papers — in short, a bundle of the factual kinds of information that help make up a person's identity.

The Star will also come with a clear idea of his goals for the day. For many of the Stars, Restoration is a day of letting go emotionally, of experiencing the love they had forgotten they had, of feeling the sadness they thought they had buried. The day will bring up many issues they did not think they had brought with them. And from this re-experiencing and re-feeling will come a new healing.

I prepare for my work with the Star by interviewing him extensively just prior to the workshop itself. The purpose of the interview is two-fold:

First, I must know the Star's life as thoroughly as possible, in order to guide him through the Restoration. I need a sense of where he might be stuck. I need a feel for areas of special sensitivity and difficulty. I need to know the old issues, the hurts, the festering wounds that he feels reluctant to bring up before the group.

Second, we need this time together in order to build the trust in each other that will make the journey a success.

Workshop participants are cast in specific roles in the Star's generational history. The casting process can be ambiguous and unpredictable, because many times the person cast in a certain role tries to deal with his own family issues inherent in that role. For example, if the Star is a man who casts me in the role of his daughter, I become a daughter again.

Daughter is one of many roles I have played in my life, but I have not been a daughter to my father for many years. As I feel myself in this role, memories come flooding back. I go with my feelings, paying attention to the situation the Star wants to recreate, and our dialogue flows. Together we re-live an event from his past, and both of us learn that in that particular situation, each person did the best he could.

A healing takes place, not just for the Star, but for the person so fortuitously cast in the role of daughter, who healed in her heart a breach with her own father. I do not know why this happens. I know only that the Star's life is a vehicle through which others can sort out their own issues and emotions.

During the Restoration, these vignettes are re-enacted all day, punctuated with pauses as the group gives feedback on various scenes. Participants may not analyze events, but instead they must concentrate on the feelings that arise during the recreations. If someone strongly identifies with an incident being staged, I encourage him to work through his feelings in demonstrative ways: Scream, move the anger up through the stomach and expel it through the mouth. Take a bataca bat and beat past hurts and rage onto a pillow. Cry. Let past sadness well and spill forth.

If we analyze a situation, we talk it over, we talk about feelings. And if we talk about what we feel, we may come up with valuable insights about feeling, **but the only way to work through feelings is to *feel*.**

The drama moves in reverse. The Star's current family is examined first, followed by his/her life in his/her family of origin and then his/her grandparents' families. Where the Star is today is not the result of random circumstances. The Star comes to view his/her life as a necessary one, as the only life he/she could have had, given the generational path cut long ago.

Wednesday, the participants split into small groups for more individualized work. By this time, we have jelled into a "family," and the small groups become very intimate. Those who surrender themselves to this feeling do the best work. In a loving, supportive atmosphere, the tears, rage, shame, pain, and ultimately the joy that people hide in order to live day-by-day — all come to the surface. For many participants, this is the most exhausting and rewarding day of the whole workshop.

Thursday, we give a special party called **The Parts Party** — another technique inspired by Virginia Satir. It's a Gestalt exercise in which one person lists his personal qualities, personifies them with well-known personalities, and casts one of the participants in each part. Then, as the "parts" sit down to a party with each other, the person walks the periphery of the "revelry," and observes the interaction.

Who dominates? Who brings the greatest joy? Who could best serve the party by leaving? As the person pauses next to each character, he may speak with them and negotiate terms under which they may stay. For example, the "comedian" at the party (often Rodney Dangerfield) may stay if he does not dominate the loving, saintly Mother Theresa.

The parts party gives the host a chance to look at himself as the sum of his parts, to love parts of himself without loving all, and conversely to reject some parts of himself without despairing that he is "all bad."

On that note, we end the workshop with the Serenity Prayer:

> *God, grant me the serenity to accept the things*
> *I cannot change;*
> *the courage to change the things I can;*
> *and the wisdom to know the difference.*

And we cling to each other for just a moment longer. The four days are over, just when they should be. And many of the participants are eager to return home to put into practice what they have experienced during the workshop.

I leave each Restoration workshop with a profound respect for the people who have risked, who have surrendered themselves to the process. And I have an abiding gratitude that my Higher Power has led me to this work.

The change in name from "Reconstruction" to "Restoration" is neither a whimsical change nor a trivial one. "Restoration" connotes a desire to return people to their "original personhood" — that is, the person they were before they adapted their behavior to accommodate a sick system. And we seek to "restore" rather than to change.

What happens for the Star of a successful Restoration? A successful Restoration ends, not when the Star's work is done, but with the Star's awareness of where the work should begin. The Star now has the choices and can make them freely and consciously.

To summarize: Through family restoration, co-dependents are able to . . .

- Study their family history;
- Relive experientially for full cognitive and emotional understanding;
- Express repressed emotions and allow the inner child to reach for support;
- Begin to trust and hope in a safe, consistent environment with people who identify and understand;
- Find a new understanding and a wider perspective as they move from subjective pain to objective clarity;
- Begin the process of forgiving others and start taking responsibility for their own well-being;
- Learn how to ask for help, affection, comfort and love, keeping in mind that for co-dependents, accepting is far more difficult than giving;
- Accept that responsibility begins a new freedom.

Self-Help Groups for Co-Dependents

In addition to formal structured treatment, co-dependents may find much understanding and support in one of the many self-help groups found in communities across the country. Adult Children of Alcoholics (ACoA) groups are leaderless support groups that vary in quality, intensity, and knowledge about co-dependency.

Al-Anon also provides help for co-dependents through ACoA meetings. In contrast to other ACoA groups, Al-Anon ACoA meetings adhere to the 12 Steps and 12 Traditions of Al-Anon.

ACoA groups have increased in phenomenal numbers in the past few years. When traditional therapists prove to be uninformed and uninterested in co-dependency issues, co-dependents turn to ACoA groups for support and help. In doing so, co-dependents make an exciting discovery: They learn that they are not alone, that they are not isolated. They learn that others have felt the pain, lived through the uncertainty and hurt and bottled-up emotions, struggled with the stress, turmoil and bewilderment of being an adult child.

Experience with any kind of therapy or self-help group shows that no single group — no one brand-name therapy — can meet everyone's needs. Co-dependents should feel free to visit different groups, shop around, until they find the one that fits.

The value of these groups cannot be accurately estimated, but few would deny that they have been of inestimable help for countless numbers of children of alcoholics and other co-dependents.

Co-Dependent Rights In Recovery

During recovery, the co-dependent focuses so much energy on feelings and relationships that the co-dependent's rights become blurred and misunderstood. I believe that it's important for the co-dependent to have some guidelines of behavior to follow in early recovery, and I have sketched out a set of suggested guidelines of personal rights:
- I have a right to say "No!" to anything that violates my values. (I do not have to passively acquiesce and defer to others when my values are at stake.)
- I have a right to dignity and respect.
- I have a right to set my own priorities and say "No!" to any request that conflicts with my priorities. (This is not a right to total selfishness, it's a right to self-care.)
- I have a right to stand up for myself. (And if I don't, I can't expect others to take me seriously.)
- I have a right to say "No!" (I have a right to be an assertive person — not confusing assertion with aggression.)
- I have a right and an obligation to show my feelings. (My feelings are part of the real me — my real response to others and to the world. And no one can read my mind to know what I feel.)

- I have a right to say, "I don't care." (I need to pass by some things, some people, and I need to be able to let go of the hurtful things in my past.)
- I have the right to change my mind. (I don't have to stick with a bad decision to the bitter end.)
- I have the right to make mistakes. (I don't have to **like** making mistakes, but I will make them, and I'm entitled to make them because, as the saying goes, no one's perfect.)

As you can see, with rights come responsibilities. And here is a paramount responsibility:

- I have the obligation not to violate these rights in anyone else.

Choicemaking

Every day I have before me many choices.
It is not easy to choose,
For often the choice means letting go
    of the past
    of the present.

I know what the past was.
I know what the present is.
But the choice propels me into the future.
I'm not sure I'll make the right choices.

It's not easy to "let go."
It's not easy to fly into the future.
It's like the space between trapezes.
It's not knowing whether you're going to be caught.
It's not knowing whether you're going to fall.

It's not easy to live in trust.
That space between trapezes requires faith.
I must admit that my faith is often shaky.

I pray and hope that I'll make good decisions,
That I'll be caught and will not fall.

Every day I have before me many choices.

To become healthy, to become whole, means that one must take responsibility for oneself. One must become a Choicemaker every step of the way. For a co-dependent who has spent years watching, weighing alternatives, afraid to make a mistake — often passively waiting for others to decide — becoming a Choicemaker can be a formidable task.

Yet Choicemaking is the foundation that recovery builds on. Choicemaking makes recovery possible.

What does Choicemaking entail? What kinds of choices must a co-dependent learn to make? There are four major areas of Choicemaking:

1. Choosing responsibility for oneself.
2. Making relationship choices.
3. Making time choices.
4. Choosing to "surrender."

Let's now take a closer look at each of these four crucial areas of Choicemaking.

Choosing Responsibility For Oneself

People tend to develop greater self-worth and ability to relate and sustain relationships when they have learned a "sense of personal responsibility and separateness" — in other words, a well-developed sense of individuality. A person with a sense of individuality has a keen self-awareness, a well-defined sense of feelings, attitudes and values. A person with this kind of awareness and sensitivity feels good enough to encourage others to have their own individuality and separateness.

When one develops one's own individuality and separateness, one's self-worth grows and the person feels good. And persons with a solid sense of self-worth want to see the ones they love to also feel good, and they encourage the individual separateness of their loved ones, as well as their own. Another way of putting it: When we develop our own individuality and separateness, we can also give others the space to grow. A mother who has found a career or vocation that makes her happy and fulfilled is much more likely to want her children to be individuals and to grow up independently.

In choosing to feel and accept responsibility for yourself, you . . .

★ Accept and express appropriately all your emotions, positive and negative alike, and make an effort to understand them. Do not fear them, and do not numb them. It's all right to feel angry and to show others that you're angry. It's all right to feel sad and to let others know your sadness. In a therapeutic setting, it's important to express fully and completely all your emotions. Part of a cathartic healing involves learning how to share necessary emotions appropriately. We need to develop a willingness to accept the **consequences** of expressing our emotions. The wife doesn't want to show rage because her husband might not accept her anger and might reject or divorce her . . . In fact, most people are probably ill-equipped — lack the emotional resources themselves — to deal with the free expression of emotions in others. The real danger with Adult Children of Alcoholics is that there is a tendency to take emotional expression as an end-point, and to use CoA groups or ACoA groups and the like as a place to unload, to take care of unfinished business, do griefwork, and so on — interminably.

★ Let your standards of conduct and sharing reflect who you really are, what you really think, and not what others expect from you.

★ Do not allow fears and inhibitions to control your life and seek ways to overcome them.

★ Look for the good in yourself, and in others as well.

★ Do not let yourself be "guilted" into action, so you won't disappoint someone's expectations of you.

★ Become more assertive, expect to be respected and taken seriously, and, at the same time, learn the difference between assertiveness and aggression.

★ Think of yourself in positive terms, and make allowances for occasional failures.

Does the Ideal Choicemaker go his/her own way alone, aloof, carefree and independent? Not at all. Choicemakers stay concerned and interested in others, but Choicemakers do not allow that concern and care to become the center of their existence. As Choicemakers we will direct our own lives as much as possible, without seeking control over others, and without letting ourselves be subservient to another's opinions or feelings.

We will learn to decide if we want to have a career or stay at home. A decision, **not** an expectation.

We will decide whether to adhere to family traditions, or start some of our own.

We will choose whether to have a career change, or stay with an early-chosen profession.

We will learn to take care of ourselves and with **care** negotiate our involvement in relationships.

As Choicemakers we won't necessarily always like what we see each other do, or what we hear each other say. But we'll feel free to share with fellow Choicemakers what we don't like for the sole purpose of sharing or enhancing understanding. We are not to remold others in our image. In respect for each other's personhood, we will let each other decide whether to change or not. Anything less in this sharing process is covered-up manipulation.

The rewards of Choicemaking are great. Novelist James Michener might have been talking about a Choicemaker when he wrote:

> *For this is the journey that men make: to find themselves. If they fail in this, it doesn't matter much what else they find: money, position, fame, many loves, revenge are all of little consequence, and when the tickets are collected at the end of the ride, they are tossed into a bin marked FAILURE. But if a man happens to find himself — if he knows what he can be depended upon to do, the limits of his courage, the position from which he will no longer retreat, the degree to which he can surrender his inner life to some woman, the secret reservoirs of his determination, the extent of his dedication, the depth of his feeling for beauty, his honest and unpostured goals — then he has found a mansion which he can inhabit with dignity all the days of his life.*

— Fires of Spring

Choicemaking *par excellence!*

Once we succeed in taking the first steps toward our own freedom in personal responsibility, we can choose to share our "self" with someone else in a relationship of our CHOICE. We won't just "**fall**" in love" with someone, we won't be mindlessly **swept** away. We will find someone we can choose to love.

As Choicemakers, we will cultivate friendships that are mutually rewarding, mutually enriching. We will learn the value of choosing to move away from relationships that bring us down, that thwart our self-worth. We will learn to abandon, if necessary, lifestyles encumbered with negative thoughts and feelings. As Choicemakers, we take the initiative to surround ourselves with individuals who bring out the very best in us, and help us in our inner journey toward goodness, love, and inner peace.

Relationships

Friendship

As Choicemakers, we will seek out persons with whom we can be fully honest — honest with our thoughts, our ideas and our emotions. We will choose friends who are easy to be around, friends who are trustworthy, friends we do not need to impress.

We will have friends who understand when we are sometimes inconsistent, sometimes negligent, sometimes too busy. **A true friend will make no demands**, will not run guilt trips on us for something we "should" have done.

Most of all, we can be quiet with a true friend. We can allow our soul to heal in the presence of a friend who is a kindred Choicemaker. We won't have to speak, nor utter a sound, but only sit quietly, while our friend occasionally smiles or reaches out to comfort us with a touch. There will also be times of hysterical laughter, a release of hilarity over little funny things — events that the rest of the world would frown at, or look on with an indulgent smile.

A true friend, a fellow Choicemaker, has a gentle heart and does not seek mastery over the lives of others. With a friend, giving and receiving come naturally and without pressure or urgency. With friends, with fellow Choicemakers, we meet person to person, mind to mind, thought to thought, heart and soul in communion.

Primary Relationship (Spouse, Mate, or Lover)

Out of one of our loving friendships, we may find a special person with whom we may want to commit ourselves in a primary relationship. Somewhere I came across the following words that seem to capture, for me, the essence of a healthy primary relationship:

Love is a friendship that has caught fire. It is quiet understanding, mutual confidence, sharing and forgiving. It is loyalty through the good times and bad. It settles for less than perfection and makes allowances for weaknesses.

Love is content with the present, it hopes for the future, and it doesn't brood over the past. It's the day-in, day-out chronicles of irritations, problems, compromises, small disappointments, big victories and common goals.

If you have love in your life, it can make up for a great many things you lack. If you don't have it, no matter what else there is, it is not enough.

Intimacy with a spouse, mate, or lover transcends the physical. Intimacy includes physical closeness and sex. But just as important, we also feel free to talk openly with each other and move closer to each other in each of the important areas of our lives: emotionally, intellectually, sexually, socially, and spiritually. Outside the pages of romance novels and TV soaps, intimacy seldom occurs spontaneously. It develops as two people come to know each other and mutually choose the setting, the milieu, in which intimacy can flourish.

Intimacy carries with it the potential for monogamy. But not everyone is capable of monogamy, not everyone can make the commitment monogamy requires. Monogamy places certain demands on the partners, and it takes two individuals of high self-worth and personal responsibility, not to mention mutual respect and flexibility, to become intimately monogamous.

Monogamy requires that two people share enough of the same interests, desires and goals to want to spend time developing an intimate relationship. It is necessary to have in common a shared vision of life's purpose and possibilities and to have the caring generosity to work together to help each other fulfill personal goals and mutual goals. Psychologist Nathaniel Branden tells his clients, "Never marry a person who is not a friend of your excitement."

A person who chooses monogamy has enthusiasm, loyalty, honesty, healthy self-worth and openness. Over time in the committed relationship, each person acquires more patience, trust and comfort.

Trust, of course, depends on honesty and faith. We have trouble trusting others in an early encounter because we have no experience with that person. We can make certain assumptions, but we have no accurate gauge of the new person's reliability, honesty, predictability, or potential for viciousness. Many people have been terribly harmed by placing trust in strangers, in new acquaintances, who turned out to be untrustworthy, sometimes dangerously so.

Trust comes as we accumulate experience with each other. The committed couple grow in trust.

In the demands that monogamy makes, persons may falter and retreat because of low self-worth, because of their inability to be honest with themselves, because of their unwillingness to work toward intimacy — or for any number of other reasons. Or persons may embark on a monogamous voyage of mutual discovery and self-transformation.

Monogamy, in perspective, does not entail a loss of self or a diminution of freedom. Instead, monogamy allows the emergence of a more true and deep self — an apparent paradox. "The more I am truly myself," the paradox goes, "the more I can be truly one with you. The more I am truly one with you, the more I can be truly myself." Thus, in monogamy, two entities become a single, higher-order entity, as the whole is greater than the sum of its parts — a transcendent entity, separate and distinct from the two constituent entities which are not lost, but retain their full individuality.

A monogamous union also provides room for sexual exploration and growth **between** the committed partners. In workshops, the question often arises, "What is the effect on the relationship when one or both of the partners have other sexual partners?" Rather than viewing extra sexual partners or affairs as a "natural" right of either person, or as a change bringing a freshness into the monogamous relationship, we should see the sexual ploy as evidence that one of the partners is avoiding change. Again, Nathaniel Branden points out that after the superficial erotic novelty has faded, after the ego has been pumped up, flattered and fed (and life stories told and sexual tricks played), the adventure will cease. And it then becomes necessary to rekindle the dying flame by locating another sexual partner.

Fervid sexual adventures blunt the sharp cutting edge of loneliness and emptiness, and temporarily divert attention from critical issues in the monogamous relationship. Immersed in the erotic, the individual loses sight of relationship values and more often than not behaves dishonestly and irresponsibly.

The rallying justification of the individual passionately celebrating sexual emancipation is: "Why should I be satisfied with a sandwich, when there's a feast out there?"

Obviously, the person who seeks the sexual feast down the primrose path of dalliance has never experienced Higher Monogamy. Casual recreational sex can hardly be called a feast — not even a good, hearty sandwich. It is a diet of non-nutritive fast food served in throwaway plastic containers.

Life's feast — life's **real** feast — is available only to those who are willing and able to engage life, to make commitments, on a deeply personal level.

Unfortunately, people make bad choices of partners. Sometimes early commitments or relationships are made when people are still in an early stage of recovery from their illness — alcoholism, drug dependency or co-dependency. As they struggle and strive to relinquish the dependency or the addictions, the relationship emerges as a major part of the illness, and hence cannot be a part of the recovery. One partner may depend on the other for financial security or emotional security or intellectual stimulation. As these dependencies are confronted and healed in treatment, partners may end up **not knowing or even liking each other.**

In other cases, both partners struggle to get well, and they emerge from the ordeal with exciting new possibilities for an intimate and fulfilling partnership. Depending on the health and willingness of both partners, the prognosis can be favorable, or it can be bleak.

Let's take a look at what lies ahead for those with a bleak prognosis and for those with a favorable one.

Spiritual Divorce

Spiritual divorce figures prominently in the bleak prognosis. A spiritual divorce occurs when a couple remain living together, keeping up a facade of harmony and a pretense of mutual satisfaction with the relationship. La Rochefoucauld once noted: "We get so in the habit of masquerading before others, that we soon appear disguised before ourselves." So it is with spiritual divorce: The couple may even come to believe the pretense and may make strenuous efforts to perpetuate the myth that High Monogamy reigns supreme.

Such marriages take a lot out of each of the partners, and children caught in these relationships undergo pain and devastation. I feel a pang of sadness whenever I hear a couple admit, "We are staying together for the good of the children." By the time this kind of admission can be verbalized, the children have usually felt the emptiness and phoniness of the marriage for a very long time. As adult children, they feel confused about what kinds of relationships they want to have, and they feel guilty about the "sacrifices" made by their parents — and the parents, with a sense of martyrdom, do nothing to assuage the guilt.

All couples go through slack times, passive times, doubtful times and hard times with each other. But these periods of doubt and questioning and dissatisfaction are transitory. The relationship remains secure.

But when the conditions become chronic, it's a sure sign that spiritual divorce has set it. Symptoms of spiritual divorce include:

- Chronic and persistent sadness between partners.
- Chronic boredom and emptiness, manifested in overeating, TV addiction, compulsive outside activities, third person relationships, and so on.
- Indifference to each other's problems, a cooling of mutual interests or excitements.
- Habitual sexual coldness.
- Lack of small courtesies and tenderness.
- Climate of insincerity and mutual mistrust.
- Superficial communication.
- Consistent feeling of being alone and misunderstood.
- Atmosphere of chronic tension and stress.
- Sarcasm, insults and an atmosphere of pervasive rudeness.
- A relationship permeated by "silent violence" (the Silent Treatment).
- Individual spiritual lives — each partner having a private God and a private spiritual search.
- Loss of the capacity for surprise and wonderment with each other.

For a contrasting perspective on relationships devoid of malaise and spiritual divorce symptoms, let's now turn to the kind of relationship that may blossom into a nourishing, loving commitment.

Loving, Committed Relationship

This type of relationship is one in which both people admit to the value of it and each other. They make a commitment to each other, a commitment to work toward intimacy and a deeper love in a monogamous state. Each person takes the responsibility to fashion a separate life, however, and each finds ways to fulfill needs without expecting the other person to meet all needs.

In a loving, committed relationship, partners **listen** to each other. They listen acceptingly and uncritically. They listen in a way that helps the troubled person reach solutions, rather than in a way that insults, demeans or impedes understanding. Instead of ignoring, they listen. And they do not try to "fix" the problem.

Each person hears what the other asks, and if it does not interfere with their own well-being, each will offer a part of himself to fulfill the request. And, in turn, they will ask to have some of their needs, wants and wishes fulfilled. Neither will stand in the way of the other's development.

Tim, a dentist, respects his wife's need to have a career. When she decided to go back to school to become a lawyer, Tim was willing to accept many role reversals concerning home care and child-rearing.

Beth spends more time alone than she chooses because her husband's inconsistent work demands keep him away. But Beth keeps busy with activities that are important and fulfilling to **her** so that her husband can feel free to do the things he chooses to do.

One of the solutions to conflict that my husband Joe and I have found is what we call our "John-file." John is a therapist/mentor who has provided us with the necessary "outside opinions" from time to time. Conflicts interrupt our good times together. So we try to resolve each conflict as it comes up. If we can — great! If we can't, however, we write each conflict down — sometimes in the wee hours of the morning — and put it in the John-file. We see John at regular intervals. By writing down our individual concerns, we both feel validated that our concerns are important to each other and won't be avoided or disregarded. Once we write and file the conflict, we get on with our relationship (eating, sleeping, talking, sharing, etc.) until we see John again. We are unwilling to let conflict interrupt our living for any significant length of time.

In a loving, committed relationship, each person will share much about their journey and spiritual quest. They will share dreams, plans, vacations, pleasure time — and the couple will share, unpressured by the other, in many of the same ventures. Each will bend a little in their separate entity to fulfill the "coupleship." And each will nurture the coupleship from their own developed selfhood. In essence, the coupleship and each selfhood exist in a symbiotic relationship, where each component enriches and enhances the other.

And when day is done, they will come together with spontaneity and delight in each other's company. They will not be embarrassed to become like children and delight in the closeness and wonderment of each other. They are truly blessed, for there is a warm and secure feeling of "homecoming" each time they are together. It is a mood vividly expressed by Anthony Padavano:

> One never comes home until one prefers a gentle heart to mastery of other lives. One comes home when one learns how to bring a gift **and** how to receive one. When one is home, he gives love, makes comfort, hurts for justice. One is homeward-bound when one is more tormented by the death of innocence than by the frustration of ambition. One makes a home every time he allows a person to feel at home with "self." One is on the right road, not far away, close enough to run the last mile, when he realizes that the greatest of all gifts to give another is home, and that the most

surprising and wonderful gift to receive is "homecoming."

We all have certain close friends, spouses, lovers — people we get together with, people who really make us feel, in their presence, that we have come home. And in this relationship, we are blessed with what we can only refer to as "homecoming."

We have looked at aspects of Choicemaking involving the areas of self-responsibility and relationships. Now, let's look at another important feature of Choicemaking — choices about time.

Choices About Time

We all have the same amount of time. We each get 24 hours every day, 60 minutes every hour, 60 seconds every minute. If we sleep an average of 8 hours a day for our lifespan — say, three score and ten — then we will have spent 204,400 hours in somnolence. That's roughly 23 years asleep. And you thought you never got enough sleep . . .

Even though we all have exactly the same amount of time each day, for some of us it isn't enough. We have too many things we'd like to do — too many good books to read, too many new electronic gadgets to master, too many experiments to do, too many high mountain trails to hike, and on and on. Time flashes by. What we need is a good 48-hour day.

And for some of us, time weighs heavy on our hands — there's too much time, and it seems to creep in its petty snail's pace, so that days become interminable. We find ways to kill time, to blot it out. We find ways to make the agonizing days bearable. Alcohol. Drugs. Television (the "plug-in drug"). Video games. Trivial Pursuit. Cards. Anything to pass the time, to fill up the dreary hours. Anything to keep from facing the banal emptiness of our lives.

There are many useful books and articles about how to save time, spend time, invent time and use time.

Time for me has become a source of great treasure, and I find I need to guard it closely or it is often stolen. A few years ago I started a practice I still continue. Very often my dates for lectures are booked two years in advance. At first, I responded to invitations with great enthusiasm, only to find myself almost snowed under with commitments six months later — sometimes working 50-60 hours a week.

I learned to sit down each January 1 and book the time I need or want for the coming year. In short, I book Sharon first. Joe and I also book "timeless time" every three months. That means a few days just for us — unscheduled. In timeless time, we do not have to answer to anyone or anything. And we find that timeless time has a healing quality of its own.

In making choices about time, I block out special times (birthdays, holidays and other special days) that are to be saved and honored. Demands on my time need to adjust to the time I have to give. This comes right down to day-to-day living. I've learned to put my time where my values are. And I'm willing to take whatever consequences that decision costs.

My clients have learned to make similar choices. Two important considerations are:

1. What do you have to let go of?
2. Who might you disappoint?

It may be necessary to detach from people or situations that consume one's time voraciously — particularly if one needs that time for self-renewal. And it might be necessary to disappoint some people who make demands on one's time.

Surrender to Choice/Choose To Surrender

Sometimes I believe that it is the Higher Power that touches us, making it possible for us to have the inner wisdom and courage to surrender. And other times, I believe that our own inner wisdom and courage invite the Higher Power into our lives. I leave you to believe whatever is right for you. However, I do know that some feelings and behaviors are necessary for contact with the Higher Power.

SURRENDER

To **surrender** means not to be protective of others.
It's to let our loved ones face their own reality, the
   consequences of their own decisions.

To **surrender** means to stop trying to control others.
It's to use my energy to become what I dream I
   can be.

To **surrender** is not to regret the past.
It's to grow and live for the future.

To **surrender** is to stop denying.
It's to become more accepting of reality.

To **surrender** does not mean to stop caring.
It means I can't do it for someone else.

To **surrender** means I cannot enable any longer.
It means I have to allow others to feel their own
   consequences.

To **surrender** means to stop being in the middle of the
   arranging of events.
It's to allow others to impact their happenings.

> *To **surrender** is to be unwilling to adjust my schedule*
> *to everyone else's.*
> *It's to take full responsibility for me.*
>
> *To **surrender** is to fear less and give up guilt and*
> *inadequacy.*
> *It's to love and accept both myself and others more.*

Surrender means "acute awareness and acceptance of reality—the acceptance that 'this is the way it truly is!' " Once we have surrendered, we make new choices from a stance of awareness.

The best statement of surrender and awareness one can make is the first step of the A.A. Twelve-Step program:

"My life has become unmanageable . . ."

Once the unmanageability is accepted, when reality is truly acknowledged and one surrenders, there are new choices to make.

Twelve Steps for Co-Dependents

The Twelve Step "way of life," carefully thought out and promulgated by early members of Alcoholics Anonymous, has helped guide the lives of hundreds of thousands of people world-wide. The Twelve Steps have been a very important part of my life, and I thank God for the inspiration that guided the work of Bill W. and Dr. Bob, the co-founders of A.A., who helped formulate the Twelve Steps.

Because of the genius and complete wisdom of these steps, many lives have been saved and restored to serenity and peace. The Twelve Steps have become models of twelve-step guides to recovery from all sorts of conditions. There are twelve steps for cancer patients, for overeaters and gamblers and drug addicts — for emotionally hurt people of all kinds.

I'm sure Dr. Bob and Bill W. would be joyful to see their work used to help so many different people in so many situations.

For a complete understanding of the Twelve Step programs, I would recommend two books:

- *Alcoholics Anonymous* (often called "The Big Book")
- *Twelve Steps and Twelve Traditions*

Both books are published by AA World Services Inc., Box 459, Grand Central Station, New York, NY 10017.

Because there are many co-dependents who will not be familiar with Twelve Step programs, I have paraphrased the steps in a way that I think will be useful for co-dependents:

1. We acknowledge and accept that we are powerless in controlling the lives of others, and that trying to control others makes our lives unmanageable.
2. We have come to believe that a power greater than ourselves can restore enough order and hope in our lives to move us to a growth framework.
3. We make a decision to turn our lives over to this power to the best of our ability, and honestly accept that taking responsibility for ourselves is the only way growth is possible.
4. We make an inventory of ourselves, looking for our mental, emotional, spiritual, physical, volitional and social assets and liabilities. We look at what we have, how we use it, and how we can acquire what we need.
5. Using this inventory as a guide, we admit to ourselves, to God as we understand him, and to other caring persons, the exact nature of what is within that is causing ourselves pain.
6. We give to God as we know Him, all former pain, hurt and mistakes, resentments and bitterness, anger and guilt. We trust that we can let go of the hurt we cause and receive.
7. We can ask **for** help, support and guidance and be willing **to** take responsibility for ourselves and to others.

8. We begin a program of living responsibly for ourselves, for our own feelings, mistakes, and successes. We become responsible for our part in relationship to others.

9. We make a list of persons to whom we want to make amends and commence to do so, except where doing so would cause further pain for others.

10. We continue to work our program, each day checking out our progress and asking for feedback from others in our attempt to recovery and grow. We do this through support groups.

11. We see through our own power and a Higher Power, awareness of our inner selves. We do this through reading, listening, meditation, sharing, and other ways of centering and getting in touch with our inner selves.

12. Having experienced the power of growing toward wholeness, we find our bodies, minds and spirits awakened to a new sense of physical and emotional relief which leaves us open to a new awareness of spirituality. We seek to explore our meaning in life by honest sharing with others, remembering that BECOMING WHO WE ARE is a lifetime task which must be done one day at a time.

I see these Twelve Steps for Co-Dependents as useful guidelines and reminders of our tasks in recovery. They are not meant to imply affiliation with A.A., Al-Anon, or any other self-help group structured around a Twelve-Step format.

7

On-Going Recovery

It is time to celebrate and rejoice in the victory of freedom from addiction and painful compulsive behaviors. We have found a program that will help us continue to free ourselves from situations and feelings that have brought us physical and emotional pain.

This victory has not been easy. It has been difficult. There has been much hard work, good-byes to say, hellos to face, new experiences, times of loneliness and times of self-doubt. New questions and wonderings have surfaced. Yet we know that we are on the right path because our lives have begun to work better, and we have started to feel an inner peace and comfort.

We have freed ourselves from chemical bondage, and we have decided to become Choicemakers. These two accomplishments allow us to make a passage, to grow. In a growth framework, there is constant, gentle, life-giving movement. To stop growing is to stagnate. If we pool and dam up the water in a river, the waters become murkish and stagnant. The river will die.

The same holds true for people. We exist to live and grow. We are alive, vital. For those who are at a point of freedom, there will be many new experiences. The next part of this book will explore that journey.

One caution: Throughout our recovery, we are faced with a dangerous temptation to rely on the Higher Power so completely that we forget that our job is to work **with** the Higher Power. We are co-creators in shaping our destinies and futures. And as co-creators, we have an active, not passive, role in our own recovery.

The Honeymoon

In traditional terms, the honeymoon is a special time of good feeling, high expectation and extraordinary closeness that follows a commitment and special event. For our purposes, the honeymoon is a time following therapy or treatment when the new information and feelings peak to generate an almost electrical aura of excitement and hope.

I believe that this is an authentic experience and that it should be enjoyed to the fullest. The good feeling of this time will be necessary to sustain the recovering person as he/she re-enters and re-negotiates future relationships.

But the recovering person must also expect to encounter some "pitfalls" during recovery. These pitfalls must be planned for and worked through in recovery. I am going to borrow from the ideas of Mary Lee Zawadski, the director of a chemical dependency program in Florida, in the following discussion of recovery obstacles.

Pitfalls Of Recovery

1. Defiance. Even though there is an acceptance of the co-dependency concepts and one admits to suffering from the illness, one may hang on to anger about the situation. One may also cling to the belief that knowledge alone can adequately treat the pathology. The recovering person says, "I know I should change, but . . ." Pay attention to what follows after the word "but" and you are likely to gain insight into that person's co-dependency. All the knowledge in the world will not heal, nor will it change behavior. Healing does not take place on an arid intellectual plane. Only surrender and emotional healing can truly balance the pain of co-dependency.

2. Secret Recovery: This is the pitfall of persons with extremely low self-worth who feel that they don't have the right to recover. They may smile knowingly in the mirror and give themselves a secret wink, or admit to themselves that they feel happier, that they have fewer problems. But they avoid letting anyone else know. No one will guess their secret and their recovery will remain shrouded in mystery. Why the mystery? Such people feel that until everyone else is happy, all personal happiness should be downplayed. These individuals are still strapped in a cumbersome, old belief system that teaches that there is something noble and admirable about suffering, struggling, or having problems. To show happiness or excitement is wrong. Those trapped in a secret recovery resist owning the **right** to health and happiness. Their conversations carry a clutter of "dis-ease" words: "could," "should," "try," and "but."

3. Emotional Binges: For one who has waited so long to feel and even longer to express those feelings, there is a danger of staying at the discharge level. To begin to feel and have an opportunity to express those feelings is a type of "detox." It's a time to rid oneself of emotional repression. However, some co-dependents get hooked on the detox and don't move into the next phase of recovery. To center recovery on emotional expression alone is very risky, because it means exchanging emotional numbness for an overdose of emotionality. When emotional expression becomes the be-all and end-all of recovery, you can be sure that the recovering person is in a rut.

4. Avoiding Change: To know that one needs to make a change and actually making the needed change are two quite separate activities. Recognizing that a change is needed takes place on the cognitive level. Making the change involves actively engaging in new behavior. Books are full of proverbial wisdom attesting to the difficulty of translating knowledge into action. (Actions speak louder than words. The spirit indeed is willing, but the flesh is weak.) Knowing that change is necessary and refusing to take the steps that lead to change result in frustration and self-recriminations. And the last thing a recovering person needs is the stress that comes with frustration.

5. Living By Mottoes or Frameworks: The recovering person can often get an "A" in therapy and an "F" in healing. Too frequently the recovering person buys a handy-dandy recovery kit from a counselor, mentor, treatment center, support group, or current social "movement." The recovery kit, it is said, has all that's needed for a full recovery — it has all the wise sayings to be memorized for stressful occasions. It has all the "right" literature written by the "right" gurus. The recovery kit has a "Bible" and it has the wisdom of the saints. In short, it has all one needs to know, if not all there is to know, for one's total recovery program. However, it's important that we remember that we are "co-healers" with our Higher Power, and that we bring to the healing process the sum of our insight, intuition and wisdom. We integrate what we "know" with what we learn and find ways to adapt both to our unique individual situation. It is a form of folly to buy any whole program, without putting any of our "self" into it. We play an active role in recovery, not a passive, receptive role alone. (At the same time, we must be wary of our tendency to "know it all," and be receptive to new learning and the wisdom of others who have been pathfinders in recovery.)

If we blunder into any of these pitfalls, we run the risk of relapse or stagnation in our growth. If we are in a vulnerable position to relapse and stop growing, we might be able to detect the following symptoms in ourselves. If we cannot see them in ourselves, at least we can be alert to the symptoms and be open to listen if someone notices our own symptoms and confronts us about them.

- **Fatigue:** Allowing ourselves to become overly tired and careless about our health.
- **Workaholism:** Usually a sign that we are less effective than we envision we "should be." Sometimes this is true because we are overly tired, and sometimes we have simply set unrealistic expectations for ourselves. Workaholism can also reflect an avoidance of dealing with intimates in one's life. The workaholic doesn't have time to share, doesn't have time to really listen to the spouse or children recite their needs. There's always work to be done, another project to start.
- **Dishonesty:** Little cover-ups, exaggerations, underestimations — all of which can grow into more elaborate forms of excuse-making.
- **Self-pity:** Beginning to believe that one is a victim of bad luck instead of taking responsibility for poor choicemaking or use of time.
- **Frustrations:** A sign that one is not feeling or expressing appropriate anger. It is also a sign that one feels blocked in one's goals, and might represent a low threshold for frustration, unrealistic expectations or poor coping skills — or all of these together.
- **Impatience:** A sign that one wants to get back into the driver's seat of control. Dissatisfaction with the pace of recovery, a feeling that things are not happening fast enough, not happening the way one wants to see them happen.

- **Relaxing the Recovery Program:** Letting up on the discipline of recovery. Not finding time for daily meditations, meetings, support groups, thinking "I'm okay now." When one forgets the mainstay of recovery, one stops recovering. Therapy groups are useful at the time of our life when we are making major life changes. We use them from time to time when needed — not as a constant lifestyle. Twelve-Step self-help groups, however, remain a consistent base of support, giving fellowship and becoming a permanent part of our recovery lifestyle.

- **Setting Unreachable Goals:** If we set goals that are unreachable, we set ourselves up for disappointment, which then leads to frustration or to self-pity. We do not set out to stay sober for the next 25 years, we set out to stay sober today. "Happiness is not having what you want, but wanting what you have."

- **Forgetting Gratitude:** You have a choice of looking at the "up" side of your life, or looking at the "down" side. It's not possible to feel gratitude and negativity at the same time.

- **Righteousness:** Often when things get better, one feels powerful, arrogant and better than those who are still struggling with their recovery. "Be not righteous over much" counseled Ecclesiastes. Unfortunately, in our righteousness we tend to find it easier to remove a speck of dust from the eye of our neighbor than to take the two-by-four out of our own.

These ten symptoms can crop up any time during recovery. We need to be vigilant. And if we detect the symptoms in ourselves, we should share with a sponsor, a friend, support group or therapist. We can nip relapse in the bud and maintain our recovery.

With an intervention and an opportunity for primary care, the person **in recovery** enters a time to face the challenges of **Healing** and **Transformation**. As a guideline to the healing process, I have put together twelve steps of healing from addiction and co-dependency.

Twelve Steps of Healing

1. **The First Step** toward healing is to make the decision to continue to seek appropriate help at each stage of healing and choicemaking.
2. **The Second Step** is to choose a wise therapist or mentor (more later on mentors) as a sponsor. It is important that this person be able to demonstrate responsible behavior in his own life. Watch for dedication to reality vs. game-playing, fantasy, or wishful thinking. There are many competent individuals as judged by worldly standards, but they are not all necessarily wise. The life of wisdom is a life of insight **combined** with action. Be sure your therapist or sponsor is a person who uses good self-care skills.
3. **The Third Step** is to dedicate oneself to truth. One needs only to speak the truth, recognizing that withholding the truth is also a form of dishonesty in which a significant moral decision is made. Recognize that people who are dedicated to truth become free from fear of exposure and are able to capture creative energy that has been buried in secretiveness, disguise and game-playing.
4. **The Fourth Step** is becoming a Choicemaker. Each time we move to new levels of personal healing, we grow, we shed the old and we gain the new. We feel grief as we give up someone, when we abandon the old, secure ways. And we feel joy when we find, at new levels of recovery, those we have a kinship with in recovery. Both grief and joy are parts of the journey of life and the further one

travels on this journey, one sees with clarity that there are increasing personal births and deaths to experience.

Spiritually healed and evolved people must continually experience the pain of change. Alcoholics, drug-dependents and co-dependents have an especially difficult time reaching health and becoming capable Choicemakers. In order to love and be loved, a person must have an identity firmly established. In a family of "dependency," separate identities are not developed. There is an entanglement of feelings and behavior — an emotionally-intertwined relationship. Co-dependency is the inability to experience wholeness or to function adequately without the certainty that one is actively being cared for by another. Dependency "needs," however, are quite all right — even desirable. Dependency needs are enjoying each other's company, liking to feel special and cared for, desiring to be stroked or touched by those we love. The need to share thoughts and ideas. The need to search for spirituality. We all have healthy needs to enjoy and have fun with each other. The pleasure of companionship and sharing are very healthy needs.

But pathological dependency is something quite different. Here are a few symptoms of pathological dependency:

• Expecting, as an adult to be cared for financially.
• Inability to tolerate aloneness.
• Lack of a sense of self-developed personal identity and self-worth.
• Wanting to be loved, rather than freely offering love.
• Expecting someone else to fix personal difficulties or conflicts.

Dr. Scott Peck calls this disorder of pathological dependency a "Passive Dependent Personality Disorder." In the diagnosis, the word "passive" is used in conjunction with the word "dependent" because the individuals concern themselves with what others can do for them, rather than what they can do for themselves. The notion of personal effort does not occur to the passive dependent. Instead, they envision an effortless passive state of receiving care, love and attention. They develop angry personalities because they regularly feel "let down" by others who can never in reality fulfill the dependent's needs or "make" the dependent happy.

This concept is an important one in co-dependent recovery because co-dependents and children of alcoholics have the responsibility to seek their **own** treatment, make their **own** risky choices, and pursue their **own** fulfillment in life — and they have the obligation to stop wallowing around in depression, sarcasm, fragility, or blame for the alcoholic family or partnership from which they came.

5. **The Fifth Step** is surrender and **taking personal responsibility** for one's own life. Some people are born into alcoholic families, and others marry alcoholics. Whether by birth or by marriage, the individual suffers certain complications of the illness. Others have similar involvement similar relationships, with handicapped persons, economically depressed persons, schizophrenics, the economically underprivileged — or with rich persons, with stoic, rigid persons.

Children and spouses have lost parents and mates through death, car accidents, emotional detachment, alcoholism and war. Others live with physical handicaps and financial disasters. There are many reasons, many causes, for loss and grief. And all of us in the human condition have issues to face and take responsibility for.

Alcoholics, co-dependents — and especially children of alcoholics — need to become responsible and surrender to their own illness and not blame history or other people for current avoidance of full responsibility.

Therapy should be used to help develop new insights and choicemaking, and to chart out paths of behavior change that put the insights and choicemaking to work. In other words, one must get on with day-to-day living.

Therapy is meant to be a roadmap — not a lifestyle.

---

6. **The Sixth Step** is to **plan a nourishing program of self-care.** We all need food and shelter, but we also need companionship, rest, fun and distraction. Dr. Scott Peck states: "Saints must sleep and prophets must learn to play." Surround yourself with people of joy. Negativity and the "poor me syndrome" are contagious, so avoid as much as possible spending time with people saturated with negative energy. We need to select a program from one of the many that are available — AA, Al-Anon, Alateen, ACoA support groups, Family Groups and others. And we should stick with it. Remember: Recovery is a process, not a destination easily reached from the freeway. And even those far along in recovery find the going tough and the road rocky and rough at times.

7. **The Seventh Step** is learning to **love judiciously.** Love is not only giving. It is the wise and judicious giving . . . and sometimes withholding. It is praising, criticizing, arguing, struggling, supporting, confronting, pushing and pulling when necessary. Judicious love is caring and supportive, but it can also mean a caring, supportive, loving, strong **confrontation.**

   The word "judicious" means "requires judgment", and knowing when to support and approve — as well as knowing when to withhold support and approval.

8. **The Eighth Step** is to **accept freedom in commitment.** Genuine love is volitional rather than emotional. One needs to choose when to focus the capacity to love. True love is not a dependency, nor is it a feeling that sweeps

us off our feet, overwhelms us to the point that we are "by love possessed."

True love involves, above all, a committed, thoughtful decision. And it is in the commitment to another that the Choicemaker finds freedom.

9. **The Ninth Step** is to **assume healthy power** in our personal lives. We often sacrifice our mental and physical God-given selves and hide in the safety of compliance and false meekness. Too frequently, recovering men and women end up with nice, smiling, empty, conflict-free relationships with mates, children, friends and a Higher Power. These superficial and intimacy-avoiding relationships make a mockery of "true friendship." Whenever I hear someone say, "We never have disagreements, everything is just fine," I know I am in the presence of one stuck in a superficial relationship. I heard a young man in A.A. one night make a statement that cut to the core: "Two things almost killed me," he said. "Being cool and always being nice."

10. **The Tenth Step** is to **choose our committed relationships** and to keep assessing them. Genuine love and commitment to friends and family, and even to our life's work are all time-consuming jobs. In addition, the most important time we can take each day is for meditation, for contact with our Higher Power and inner power. Our commitments take energy and time, and thus we should choose our relationships wisely. We must be selective. We must simplify our time and our commitment to relationships. It helps to realize that genuine love is precious and best spent on those who will accept and return it. A recovering Choicemaker cannot afford emotional clutter.

11. **The Eleventh Step** is to **accept and honor aloneness.** There's a difference between **aloneness** and **loneliness.** Loneliness is a feeling of separation from others, a sense of forlornness and utter isolation. Lonely people feel like

no one cares. They feel like aliens, cut off from communication with others on **any** level. Aloneness, however, is the unavailability of someone to communicate with at one's level of awareness. Those who travel the furthest on the road to recovery, those whose path becomes a spiritual one, will experience many times the feeling of aloneness. There are fewer people with whom we can share a mutual understanding as we grow. In time of selective aloneness, when there seems to be no one to share with, we always have the opportunity to make meaningful contact with our Higher Power. Loneliness handicaps recovery and growth. Aloneness accompanies recovery and growth, and can be seen as a **prerequisite** for communion with a Higher Power.

12. **The Twelfth Step** is to be **open to serendipity.** Serendipity is "the gift of finding valuable things not sought for." (Grace is a form of serendipity.) The person open to serendipity has a trust and a willingness to let things happen. It requires that we give up control, that we have patience and keenness of vision to recognize serendipity when it occurs. For those in waiting, serendipity happens. We do not labor to cultivate the serendipitous. Serendipity finds us.

SUMMARY

The Twelve Steps of Healing

1. Seek appropriate help.
2. Select a wise therapist or sponsor.
3. Dedicate yourself to the truth.
4. Become a Choicemaker.
5. Accept responsibility for yourself.
6. Plan a self-care program.
7. Love wisely.
8. Commit yourself.
9. Claim your personal power.
10. Assess your relationships.
11. Honor aloneness.
12. Open yourself to serendipity.

8

Barriers to Recovery

Earlier I discussed "pitfalls" that occur during the "honeymoon" of recovery, pitfalls that undermine and sabotage recovery and render us vulnerable to relapse. And I also noted that recovery, even in later stages, is not an easy road.

The way to healing exists and it's available to everyone. Yet many of us get stuck in our recovery process. We may glide around the honeymoon pitfalls, only to find that we encounter even more formidable barriers to recovery.

• **The old belief in the scarcity principle:** There isn't much, and I should be satisfied with what I have. Friends are scarce. Security is hard to come by. Love is rare. There aren't many job opportunities. There isn't enough money.

People often avoid change because they are afraid to be dissatisfied with their current situation. Fear of abandonment remains a threat for many during recovery. "I'd better stay in this relationship," the person thinks. "No one else has ever really loved me. I'd rather be satisfied with what I have than seek what I want or need—or I might end up with nothing at all." Something is better than nothing.

It is important to keep in mind that Choicemakers have innumerable possibilities, countless ways to enrich health and to enhance the ability to think. Choicemakers have the right to love, the ability to ask, and, above all, the ability to make choices. If you are filled with gratitude for what you have, you will feel abundant. And you cannot feel abundance and scarcity at the same time.

• **Guilt holds people back:** Guilt is a common barrier to recovery. I see three kinds of guilt during recovery: useful guilt, crippling guilt, and recovery guilt.

Useful guilt occurs when one has committed an offense, done something against community standards. This includes suppressing another person mentally, spiritually, or physically. Useful guilt can also come about when one denies another person the support they need to believe in themselves.

Crippling guilt is a kind of psychological burden that comes when others attempt to control you and try to make you responsible for their lives. Crippling guilt is fermented by the parent or spouse who says, "Go on out and have a good time without me, and don't worry about my being alone here. I'm used to it." A child can foster crippling guilt in a parent by saying, "I am the way I am because of your drinking— and I can't change."

Recovery guilt manifests itself in recovery by the person thinking, "I can't get any better than my family. I caused their illness, and If they can't, or won't get help, then I don't deserve to be fully happy."

To escape the guilt trap, you must first assess what it is that you truly feel. What are the guilt feelings? Where did they originate? Do you feel real guilt, useful guilt? If you've committed a wrong, then do whatever you can to make amends. Be direct, be clear, be sincere. Do what you honestly can and then accept the fact that you may not be able to make total amends — but neither can you carry around an unreasonable burden of guilt forever. Once the amends are made, release it. You can do no more. And there is much yet to be done in recovery. Get on with it.

Where the guilt is false, where it is crippling guilt or recovery guilt, you must recognize that what you have been calling guilt is really hurt and anger. Admit the hurt and anger. Feel the hurt and anger. And know a fundamental truth: <u>you cannot heal hurt and anger by calling them guilt.</u> When you risk expressing the hurt, and then expressing the anger, you will find that what you have called "guilt" disappears. The feeling was really misplaced rage covered by avoidance.

• **Fear of risk:** We risk when we act in the face of possible injury, damage or loss. There are hazards. There is uncertainty. But we often fail to realize that behind each risk lurks an opportunity to learn, a chance to advance, to grow. Fearful of the hazardous rocks in the sea, we hold back and miss the boat that sets out for new horizons. However, we can learn either through loss of the risk or through its fulfillment. <u>Change is the teacher.</u>

The unwillingness to risk is what we call security. In reality, security resides with the only constant — the Higher Power, the Divine Plan and the Spiritual Word. Once this is understood and accepted, you will find a Freedom To create whatever you want. You are free to give up and risk what is comfortable and familiar, for what is unfamiliar and perhaps uncomfortable, but challenging and potentially satisfying, fulfilling, and exciting. Scary? Awesome? Terrifying? Perhaps. But if you believe in Divine Order, you can move beyond your comfort zone.

In moving beyond the comfort zone, one can also make use of a *"Co-Creator's Tool Kit:"*

> 1. Take action, even if you fear failure. If you make a wrong choice, the consequence is simply that you have to keep making choices. (And choosing not to choose is a passive decision.)

2. Keep expressing feelings appropriately, and keep listening to others.

3. Be the first to say "I'm sorry." And move beyond grudges and old resentments.

4. Try new behaviors. New tasks, new challenges, new leisure activities — all help jog our thinking and old habits.

• **Unfinished Business:** It has been said that if there were only a half-hour left on the planet, the telephone lines would be clogged and highways would be congested with people rushing to say their last "hellos" or "good-byes." People would frantically try to contact others in their lives to say, "Remember that I love you" or "You are forgiven."

Much grief would be spared if people would make their messages clear and get on with it, rather than trying to go forward with 100 lbs. of unfinished business strapped to their backs. What does it mean to finish Unfinished Business and get on with it? <u>It means conveying clear messages in relationships and making courageous decisions.</u>

A subtle form of damage occurs in a relationship when we procrastinate, when we dawdle and leave conflicts unresolved. We become estranged from partners, from our mates. Parents become estranged from their children. Here are some guidelines for resolving conflicts and to help finish Unfinished Business.

1. Tell each other that the goal of resolving issues is that you desire greater intimacy, not to ferret out the real guilty party, not to find someone to be culpable, not to establish once and for all who's right and who's wrong.

2. Be very specific and honest about whatever problems you want to resolve. Secrets, hidden information and waiting for automatic resolution are all blocks to working through conflict, impediments to closeness and intimacy. It's a "safe" style

of dealing with Unfinished Business, not an effective one.

3. Once you start talking, be clear about what you want, and start an immediate behavior change from your position. For people in crisis, talk has been, and continues to be, cheap. Behavior change comes first and is followed by trust and hope. Be clear in stating your own expectations and be clear about what expectations you can fulfill. Each time the same problem is rehashed and old behavior continues, mistrust and hurts go deeper. If this occurs too often, respect and love suffer irreparable harm.

Finishing Unfinished Business through sharing, confrontation and support helps each person grow into an increased awareness of reality. This work with each other in trust with a Higher Power is the "**Process of Transformation.**" Untransformed persons pay a terrible price for the illusion of safety. The transformed person becomes *free*.

In freedom, one is ready and able to make commitments. I believe that commitment in primary relationships, friendships, and life's work is very important. Commitment enables one to tap into a transforming power that brings the greatest comfort, peace and belief in oneself.

> **The meeting of two personalities is like the contact of two chemical substances — if there is a reaction, both are transformed.**

• **Over-Extension:** This is another common barrier to recovery. Many persons use work, business, "busy-ness" and activity to avoid self-assessment of responsibilities and to smother the many feelings that surface during recovery. Sometimes we even use our recovery program's busy-ness to avoid what is happening in our close relationships. The busy-ness in a recovery program is easy to justify and the time used up is easy to explain. And, after all, the people around a recovering person are so happy that recovery is taking place at all that they'll put up with recovery busy-ness and avoidance of intimacy. For a while. Then undercurrents of dissatisfaction begin popping up, and there's Unfinished Business to take care of, but the recovering person has a meeting tonight . . . Perhaps tomorrow? Perhaps.

Chronic and compulsive activity is the major defense in co-dependency. Internal static (anxiety) keeps one from being able to see and feel clear enough to make risky choices.

In one of Lewis Carroll's classic fantasies, *Through the Looking Glass*, the Red Queen said to Alice: "Now here, you see, it takes all the running you can do to keep in the same place. If you want to get somewhere else, you must run at least twice as fast as that." The over-extended person feels like he must run as fast as he can just to keep a hold on recovery. To risk full recovery would mean that he would have to run twice as fast, and, of course, that's out of the question. The irony is, recovery requires stillness and quiet.

Is there a way around these barriers to recovery? I think there are many ways around the barriers, as long as one knows beforehand that the pitfalls and barriers will be found along the path to recovery. I have indicated other ways of overcoming the barriers and pitfalls in my discussion above. But there's one strategy I haven't mentioned yet. Above all, one must . . .

SIMPLIFY

Back when I was in early recovery, one of my first mentors told me that in **all** times of conflict or fatigue, I should remember one word: SIMPLIFY. Later, when I underwent many significant life changes and my life began changing for the better, I found that I still experienced stress, conflict and fatigue.

I wondered why. It didn't seem fair. Another mentor told me, "Your first lesson is still true. Simplicity is still the answer. Only it gets harder as life gets better!" When we must choose between good things and people, rather than between bad and good, it becomes much more difficult to make a choice.

Sometimes it helps to have a few, short, workable guidelines to help simplfy the process of recovery on a day-to-day basis. Try out the following suggestions. I think you'll find them useful.

- Find your particular talent — and use it.
- Think well of yourself — you have your inner knowing. Trust it.
- Be honest with yourself and others. It wastes energy to be negative, to play games or to compete for control.
- Live enthusiastically — it fosters health. It's your choice to live in constant gloom or as a realistic optimist.
- Live simply. Do not allow material possessions to possess you. Good health and an honest heart are enough.
- Have faith. Try not to worry about your problems. Worry is an exaggerated sense of your responsibility and it represents a lack of faith in your inner resources.
- Work hard. Try to discern your special gifts to the world and carry your share of the work. Back up your prayers with real personal effort.
- Play. It's the foundation of joy.
- Pray. It brings inner peace and quiet.
- Celebrate your "recovery!" Sometimes there is nothing more to do than to celebrate. The rehearsal for life is over, and the show is on . . .

REMEMBER: **Choicemaking and risk are scary . . .**

> **Laugh often**, someone might call you a fool.
> **Cry often,** someone might call you sentimental.
> **Reach out to others**, and you risk involvement.
> **Expose your feelings,** and you might get taken advantage of.
> **Love,** and you risk rejection.
> **Live,** and you risk death.
> **Hope,** and you risk disappointment.
> **Try**, and you risk failure.

. . . However:

If you risk nothing, nothing will be gained. The greatest barrier to recovery, after all, is the dogged determination to take no risks. Riskless, you avoid short-term discomfort, you avoid uncertainty and anxiety. But, riskless, you also block learning, feeling, changing, loving, and living to the fullest. **That** represents a forfeiture of human freedom.

And only the person who risks is free. And authentic personal freedom opens the door to true spirituality.

Recovery and personal healing take place when you can feel a new awareness, a sense of courage, a renewed faith and open.

And it only happens . . .

ONE DAY AT A TIME.

9

Transformation

(A Framework for Understanding Growth During Recovery)

Recovery does not "happen" once and for all. We recover over time, through a complex mosaic of interactions with other people and with our environment — our work, our living and leisure space, our spiritual affinities. And always, we make choices, decisions triggered by what happens around us and within us.

Each significant move in our recovery appears to take place in a kind of progression of events:

First, we are aware of a belief or dogma about a certain value of situation. (I have used "Marriage" and "Institutionalized Religion" in the examples that follow.) This belief has both reality and meaning for us. And we are prepared to defend it because it is a truth we hold dear.

Example: "Marriage is good."
          "Belonging to the church is good."

Second, the ego is involved in this belief because there is a personal investment. It may stem from tradition, family styles, religion or society. One's ego and self-worth are closely tied to the belief, which makes the belief take on an extraordinary value.

Example: "Marriage is good and should last forever."
"I am nothing without the church."

Third, a problem erupts — a conflict takes place. The belief no longer works. It is seen to be myth or fantasy. Disillusionment sets in and one feels shattered.

Example: "The marriage isn't working."
"I feel stifled by the hypocrisy I see, and I feel like God has abandoned me."

Fourth, there is no hope. THE END. It's over. Nothing more can be done to preserve the cherished belief. Surrender . . .

Example: "A divorce takes place."
"My church rejects me or I reject my church."

Fifth, the struggle begins. The intensity of this painful time is directly related to the amount of energy spent clinging to the old order, desperately trying to make it work. New knowledge hovers on the threshold of awareness, but old definitions, deeply entrenched thoughts, and fear prevent the new knowledge from taking hold.

Example: "I'll always be lonely and alone."
"I'll never feel close to God again or find another meaningful religious experience."

Sixth, new information seeps in and new energy and possibilities bubble under the surface. Out of the pain, some new life in another direction is building. During this time, new channels of thought and feeling are being developed within to hold the growing new awareness and expansion of consciousness. Concentration on a problem restricts energy and it constricts Choicemaking. Surrender allows new energy to flow into newly-developing channels of thought and feeling. Surrender allows expansion of opportunities and options.

Caution: Sometimes we give credit to the setting a person is in when these new experiences are taking place. We credit a new therapist, a new group, a religion, a mentor, and so on. We then tend to associate the new experience — which really belongs to the self — with external factors.

> Example: "I do have some friends and good relationships in my life."
> "Maybe God can be found in more places than church alone."

Seventh, externalization occurs, a time of opening up, sharing with trusted others. There is a feeling of joy and excitement to share this experience, and to be heard and understood by others. This validation helps make the experience real.

> Example: "I'm making new friends and starting new activities."
> "I'm meeting holy people, and I'm feeling an inner comfort."

Eighth, integration . . . At this stage, the new reality becomes part of oneself. There is a feeling of relief in the changes and a sense of inner peace. Integration, personal harmony, a sense of self-containment — this process represents growth and recovery, and it sets the stage for moving to new levels of recovery.

> Example: "I can take care of myself and trust for the best."
> "I'm finding spirituality is bigger than religion, and I'm feeling closer to God."

These patterns will repeat each time a recovering person goes through a transforming event. Let's take another look at the transformations — this time dealing with changes that take place around careers:

> 1. Basic dogma, value or belief: "Careers define much about a person." (A man is his work; or, A man's work is his life.)
>
> 2. Personal investment: "My career is me, my job or profession is crucial to my whole existence."
>
> 3. Conflict: "My job is less meaningful than it used to be. I feel stuck and bored. I'm not getting anywhere."
>
> 4. The end: "I leave my job, or I get laid off or fired. The bottom falls out, and I'm adrift."
>
> 5. The struggle: "I'll never have a good job (or a prestigious, well-paying, exciting position) again. I'm doomed to menial labor."
>
> 6. New directions, new energies: "There are more jobs and opportunities than I thought there were. My situation isn't hopeless after all."
>
> 7. Externalization: "I really like what I'm doing — I'm more excited, more creative, and much more self-confident."
>
> 8. Integration: "My happiness in work depends on how I feel about it, and I'm much more content and happy now, and far more aware of my strengths."

The transforming person lives a life of opportunity, awareness and freedom. The untransforming person exists in a stage of monotonous conformity, stuck and stunted and fearful of change. In the chart below, I highlight some of the salient characteristics of transforming persons and contrast them with untransforming persons.

Contrasts in Transformation

Transforming Persons	Untransforming Persons
Resist conformity	Conform to others
Invent new lifestyles	Act like victims
Have creative personalities	Are followers
Define own goals	Have poorly defined goals
Are directed by inner self	Other-directed
Believe personal experience	Believe what others believe
Live in the present	Live in the past or future
Accept pain as necessary	Hide from pain
Become whole	Remain fragmented
Have solid value systems	Contradictory values
Are direct and simple	Confused and complicated
Are decisive	Indecisive
Feel free	Feel stuck and powerless

In relationships with friends, mates and especially with the Higher Power, we can see the characteristics which separate transforming persons from untransforming persons.

Relationships and Transformation

Transforming Persons	Untransforming Persons
Liberating and freeing	Manipulative and controlling
Honest	Deceptive
Risking	Safe and conforming
Initiator and co-creator	Joiner and follower
Independent love	Mutual dependence
Original	Conventional
Accept love as a relationship we create	Believe we "fall" in love
Find commitment exciting and fulfilling	Find commitment restricting
Shared spirituality	Embarrassed by spirituality

As you can see, spirituality plays a large role in the transforming of a person's life. French philosopher and theologian, Tielhard de Chardin, was himself a transforming person who wrote:

> *The longer I live, the more I feel that true repose consists in "renouncing" one's own self, by which I mean making up one's mind to admit that there is no importance whatever in being "happy" or "unhappy" in the usual meaning of the words. Personal success or personal satisfaction are not worth another thought if one does achieve them, not worth worrying about if they evade one or are slow in coming. All that is really worthwhile is action — faithful action, for the world, and in God. Before one can see that and live by it, there is a sort of threshold to cross, or a reversal to be made in what appears to be man's general habit of thought, but once that gesture has been made, that freedom is yours, freedom to work and love.*

Transformations as Day-To-Day Miracles

Miracles happen when one looks honestly at a chaotic marriage, at personal fragmentation, at parent/child conflicts, at addiction to chemicals and dependency behavior. Miracles happen when one looks honestly at violence (noisy or silent) in relationships, at workaholism, and the miracle that happens is that we begin to move through the process of transformation.

A miracle took place when a mother and daughter looked into each other's eyes and admitted their sorrow and pain over misunderstandings that happened years ago. They held each other and forgave each other.

A miracle happened when a father and son both accepted their addiction to alcohol and drug treatment and went through treatment together.

A miracle happened when two spouses forgave each other all past hurts and conflicts and started over completely fresh.

A miracle took place when a teenage girl felt her first spiritual awakening when someone really listened to her pain for the first time.

A miracle took place when a man finally wept and accepted his father's death of many years ago.

A miracle happened when a lady looked at herself in the mirror for the first time and liked herself. She forgave herself for her behavior during her addictive illness.

Miracles happen again and again wherever and whenever people say "Yes!" to chaos and pain, and move outside themselves searching for redemption. Whenever the transforming person, the Choicemaker, meets a challenge, a miracle takes place — an everyday miracle.

To see the miracle-making potential in everyday life, it may help to take a new look at some old spiritual terms. I have redefined "Chaos," "Commitment," and "Redemption" to clarify their role in transformation.

Chaos: The chaos we all feel at times, the struggles that each of us faces in family life, work and relationships — the loneliness and tension-filled days and fretful nights that never seem to end — these forms of chaos are really opportunities to find our Higher Power.

Commitment: As each of us tries to grope our way through the dark and gloomy night of chaos, we can commit ourselves to the meanings we find in each situation. We are Choicemakers, and we can choose to illuminate our human condition.

Redemption: As we discover our meaning, as we make the choices we have to make in whatever the situation calls for, we have an opportunity to co-create change with the Higher Power. We are partners in day-to-day miracle-making.

With these concepts in mind, we can see now that if we go through life denying our chaos — denying ourselves the pain of awareness and risk — then we also deny ourselves the possibility of connecting with our spirit in personal redemption. If we continue to avoid our feelings of anger, rage, fear and hurt, we consign ourselves to a safe life, with day-to-day aimlessness, triviality and boredom.

Choicemakers take the challenges transformation brings. Choicemakers become co-creators in the design and production of day-to-day miracles.

Mentors and Transformation

Transforming individuals frequently encounter mentors who help make the journey easier. Guidance is very important for the traveler on the road to spirituality. Each person has a unique path to self-realization. Each person has a unique connection with the Higher Power.

But much can be learned from the journeys of others. Pitfalls can be avoided, barriers can be circumvented and mistakes can be detoured. When an encouraging guide maps out the way, the path becomes clearer and the destination seems more certain and attainable. And with the map drawn from the guide's own life and journey — with the wisdom of our mentor's experience shared in trust — we can more readily discern the option open to us, and we can make more knowledgable decisions suited for our needs.

We need all the options possible for our growth. We live in times where information and knowledge are growing experientially in all fields. We need to make ourselves aware of the new information in religion, physics and medicine. We need to listen to scientists, mystics, psychologists, executives, physicians, philosophers and others who have contributed to the ferment in the information explosion.

At the same time, we must go inward to our inner child and to our intuitive connection with the Higher Power, and we must listen carefully to our own experience and knowledge.

Knowledge plus experience equals wisdom. Wisdom and support from our mentor facilitate our action, smooth the way for transformations. We need two kinds of mentors: We need lovers — those who love us unconditionally and offer support. And we need teachers — those who confront us, forcing us to see ourselves realistically.

One of my blessings has been in having many wonderful mentors over the years. In my other writings, I have mentioned Irene and Wheelock Whitney as early and important mentors in my career. And it was Virginia Satir who opened up a whole new realm of possibilities for me. I will be forever grateful for the guidance, support, love and understanding they have given me.

In addition to professional mentors, I have also been blessed with personal mentors:

GRANDMOTHER

I don't remember her in any age frame, other than "older." Most of what I remember are her little lines of wisdom which she would explain precisely under the right circumstances. She used to say, "I just go along with what's happening." And, in her own way, she taught me to accept what is, and what comes along.

She also told me, "Remember, little girl, you're no better than anyone else. But you are always just as good." I used to think of her when I wanted to try something new. I always believed that she truly thought I could do it, and eventually, I, too, came to believe that I could do it.

MY AUNT

She was a very special lady. Very pretty and filled with kindness. As a little girl, I wanted to grow up to look stylish and fashionable the way she did. I also watched her relationship with my uncle, and I knew I wanted to experience love the way they did. I admired the way she could look, cook, smile, love — and I wanted to be a woman just like her. She taught me pride in femininity and encouraged me to like myself.

MY UNCLE

He believed I could work harder and accomplish more than I ever thought I could. He gave me strength and confidence because he treated me like someone of value. He didn't let the fact that I was young or female, or a small-town person influence his behavior or diminish my accomplishments. He knew that I could do anything that felt important to me. I have felt his support for many years.

MY MOTHER

Watching my mother's life over the years, I saw so many times that she persevered where I might have given up — given up in fatigue, discouragement, sadness or hurt. Yet, she kept coming through with a zest for life and a love for people. She has taught me courage and unconditional love. Her giving was not that of a martyr — my mother gave out of her love, her geniune Godly goodness.

MY PRIEST

He may not even know that he helped me. He was not a self-conscious mentor. But many years ago, he listened to volumes of my scrambled, disjointed sentences and reflected what he heard. During a time of major transition and transformation, he listened without judgment and helped me make sense of my experience. He taught me belief in myself and in my interpretation of experience.

MY CHILDREN

No discussion of mentorship would be complete without adding what I've learned from my children. What a blessing it was for me when a very holy man suggested to me that I continue to learn from those younger than I (and stay close to the child within) in the same proportion that I learned from my elders.

The morning that my first child was born, I was enraptured with a peak experience, a time when I felt through and through that I was a co-creator with the Higher Power.

It was four o'clock on a very dark and cold November morning. I gazed out of the window at the lights of the city, and I felt small and insignificant. The nurse entered my room and placed in my arms a little bundle wrapped in a blue blanket. I looked into the face of a new human baby — my baby — and realized that a new life existed on this earth, and that I was a part of the great chain of being. I was awed by the vibrations of connectedness and pride that I felt in my co-creation with my God. In that moment, I knew for sure who I was and why my life had meaning. My child, my newborn son, taught me meaning.

Later, when I gave birth to my first daughter, it was another entirely new experience. She felt like mother, daughter, sister, and friend. A kindred female linked with me into all eternity. As she grew older, the link remained, even though she grew in different directions from me. She became her own individual, different from me in looks, in temperament, in interests and in personality. She filled in many of the pieces that I didn't have. She taught me patience, persistence, gentleness, and contentment. Instead of being my child only, she became a role model mentor.

In contrast, my youngest daughter was, and continues to be, my carbon copy in many ways. My respect for her grew as she went through a major crisis when she was eleven years old. I watched how she struggled, then survived, and I learned from her. Later, I observed how she turned adversity into internal power. Seeing her strength, seeing myself in her, gave me much determination and humility.

My blessings in being a mother are that I have had superb mentorship from my children.

A DEAR FRIEND

I have noted with increasing wonderment how much bigger my God or Higher Power seems to become as I meet "Godly" people in my everyday life. Once when I was going through a crisis in a relationship, I went to visit a friend. I told her all the painful things that were happening in my relationship and asked her if I should go or stay. In her wisdom she said to me, "Very simple — either you commit yourself to staying, and one by one work through the problems that are present. Or you commit yourself to leaving, and one by one work through the problems that result from that decision. The solution is in the commitment, and the pain and anxiety is in the wavering. If the relationship has enough value, stay. If it's taking away too much of you, leave."

My friend showed me that I couldn't do anything about the problem until I had made a clear and definite commitment about what direction I wanted to take. She taught me how to face reality.

As you can see, I don't believe that we must latch on to a mentor who promises to cure us, or to save us, or to single-handedly lead us out of the wilderness into a land of plenty. Transforming people and Choicemakers do not become disciples to a guru who teaches one immutable truth.

In my life, I have found that I'm a little bit of all that has happened to me, and a little bit of **who** has happened to me. A man by the name of Anthony Padavano wrote some beautiful books on life, relationships, love and God. I'm sure he does not have any idea of the impact he has had on my life over the past ten years. Yet his inspired words continue to be a part of my own transforming experiences.

More recently, I have been influenced by the writings of Dr. Scott Peck, whose knowledge and wisdom about human behavior and relationships have been a constant source of inspiration and pleasure.

As I look back, I am filled with gratitude for the masterpiece I am, and I appreciate the many people who contributed to my Being. I thank God for allowing me this treasure of development.

Each of you is a special masterpiece as well. And each has encountered the help and guidance of mentors. In this section, I've wanted to jog your memory, to stimulate your thinking about the people who have served as guides and inspirations. Give yourself a treat, and think about them. Or better yet, visit them or give them a call.

Explore your life and see how you've prospered and continue to grow through mentorship. Explore, and enjoy yourself.

The Importance of Balance

One of the important lessons I have learned over time is the value of balance in transformations. Transformations can be unsettling experiences. We get so excited about our new smorgasbord of possibilities and options that we become gluttons in our eagerness to sample what life has to offer. Famished, we are tempted by the feast. We lose sight of the path we have traveled. And we become imbalanced in our recovery.

When we have balance, we have a sense of proportion, a sense of poise and equilibrium in activities and preoccupations. We don't, for example, become "recovery groupies" or "transformation junkies." A thread of harmony runs through our lives and we keep in front of us at all times the knowledge that there are different levels of consciousness available to us in spiritual growth. Many masters, spiritual teachers, mystics and sages have commented on varieties of spiritual growth and levels of spiritual consciousness. The different versions have much in common, as seen below.

1. **Survival:** The most basic awareness, the drive for self-preservation. Alcoholics and other addicts often suffer at this very basic level as they self-destruct with chemicals, food, smoking, gambling, and so on.

2. **Emotional Awakening:** Self-gratification, being able to feel. Co-dependents often suffer at this level, responding to circumstances by repressing feelings of painful experiences.

3. **Intellect:** Concerned with producing thoughts and ideas, able to analyze and understand. Professionals often suffer at this level, because they have been trained to believe that science and knowledge are the only kinds of truth that count.

4. **Acceptance:** The ability to accept and forgive ourselves and others. Recovering people have difficulty here, because they do not want to give up resentments or the myth of "what was." Or they don't want to relinquish their perception of "how it should be." They often prefer conflict.

5. **Clarity:** This is the development of some inner natural knowing. Recovering people are often afraid to trust their intuitions.

6. **Love:** This is the consciousness of being able to love, even in areas where love is not acknowledged, accepted or returned. Without the gift of faith and connection with the Higher Power, one risks becoming a controller with love, feeling as though love and love alone will suffice. In doing so, one forgets the crucial connections of the "co"-Creator.

7. **Enlightenment:** The perception of connectedness with God, with the Higher Power. Being at home in the universe. The danger comes in forgetting that it takes all levels in operation in order to achieve this level. In a word, it takes **Balance.**

As people undergo transformations and move to different stages of spiritual consciousness, there's a tendency to feel as if they're climbing "higher." Spiritual consciousness, however, is not an ordinary ladder. Paradoxically, when one's on a "higher rung" of spiritual consciousness, one is also simultaneously on each of the so-called "lower rungs." In fact, there is no "higher" and "lower" in spiritual consciousness. It encompasses all levels, it is all-inclusive.

The celebrated guru who professes to have reached Enlightenment has not moved closer to God-consciousness if all other levels are not in operation. He remains unenlightened.

Father Joseph Martin captures the essence of Balance, when he tells people, *"If I'm in a car accident, for goodness' sake, don't take me to group therapy. Take me to a hospital!"* We are mortal beings, as well as spiritual beings, and we have to live IN the world. Our job is to live IN the world. If God wanted us all to live only in the world of higher consciousness and evolution, he would take us to that place. He wants us to have the experience of "fully living." That means feet on the ground, and solid with Him, and fully experiencing everything in between.

MEDITATION

The gathering of the enlightened is slowly growing. In this growth, there is always progress among the few who are out ahead of the crowd. If you keep on striving for something better in your life, there will be no stagnation. Enlightenment is yours for the asking. Do not spend time over past failures. Count the lessons learned from failures as rungs on the ladder of progress. Keep going. Those working through dependency issues will remember a vague restlessness, a feeling that there was something more, something to be discovered, something that would satisfy. The compulsion to put certain substances first in our lives was, I believe an action taken to fill up this space, this **emptiness inside.**

10

The "God-Hole" — A Personal Spiritual Void

An inner emptiness may extend even into recovery for the recovering addict and the co-dependent alike. I believe that this void is in reality a spiritual vacuum, and we will remain restless, compulsively searching for "fixes," for solutions for our inner emptiness.

And our inner emptiness will persist and our search will continue until we are touched by spiritual awakening and, through the Higher Power, find ourselves filled with a sense of purpose and serenity.

What is spirituality after all? It is a quality that infuses life with meaning. It energizes our lives and ultimately provides us with a rationale for life and death.

Intellect, science, technology — these can all tell us how to effectively and efficiently use our bodies and our minds. They help us with the how of existence, but they offer little help in giving us the whys we yearn for. Why the rush? Why the pain and turmoil? Why the loneliness and emptiness? Intellect, science and technology remain silent. The answers will be found in another arena — the spiritual arena.

"But if I just keep busy ... or have enough to look forward to ... or follow all the traditions and do everything I 'should'—then surely my life will be happy and fulfilled. Surely it will have meaning."

Will it? Don't count on it.

I'm reminded of a lady I met a while back. She was about seventy pounds overweight. She invited me in for coffee and started telling me what a hectic week she had had. She had been busy shopping, spent too much money, was out of sorts with her husband — but she had one more gift to get and she would be done for Christmas. All she had left was cards and food.

I asked her if she was enjoying herself. She looked surprised, as if to say, "What does that have to do with anything?" However, she did tell me that she felt guilty being away from her children. And she felt resentful over the money spent. And she wished the holidays were over so she could relax.

She seemed completely caught up in what she should be doing and didn't know why she was doing any of it. I returned home feeling sad for the emptiness and powerlessness my friend had shared with me.

In contrast, another friend called me on Thanksgiving Day to wish me happy Thanksgiving. She told me that she and her husband were alone for dinner that day, but what a glorious day it was. Her life brimmed with meaning and purpose, so that to stay home, to be alone, was a time of real thanksgiving for her. It was a day to take time to be grateful for the rest of the year. A time to appreciate the abundance of happiness. She reflected true inner peace. And this inner peace is what I call the work of the Spirit.

The work of the Spirit goes by many names, and many sensitive and astute persons have, in their own spiritual consciousness, given witness:

• From Jewish writings: *When a person is singing and cannot lift his voice, and another one comes and sings along, the first will be able to lift his voice. That is the secret of the bond between spirits.*

• From William James: *We and God have business with each other through the spirit, and in opening ourselves to God and each other, our deepest destiny is fulfilled.*

• From Dag Hammarsjkold: *God does not die on the day we cease to believe in a personal God, but we die on the day our lives cease to be enlightened by the wondering about the source of all creation.*

• From the Talmud: *Man will hereafter be called to account for depriving himself of all the good things the world has to offer.*

• From Jesus Christ: *The Kingdom of God is within you.*

Someone once told a story exemplifying the mysterious way of the Spirit: When God wants an important thing done in His world, or a wrong righted, He acts in a roundabout fashion. He never lets loose with lightning or stirs up earthquakes — He has a baby born.

In this simple parable, we have a hint of meaning for our own lives. Each of us is a baby, born to a life of challenge, born to a life of Choicemaking and transformation. And it is up to each of us to remain open to the Spirit, to the challenges of spiritual transformation. There are many who speak the truth of the Spirit and, surrendering, we too join with them, and celebrate the truth of the Spirit and the serenity it brings.

"But how does one learn about the Spirit?" Not through long hours spent perusing erudite tomes on Fundamentals of Spirituality. Nor by sitting through two semesters of "Spirit 101 and 102: Survey of Spirituality." It is not a mysterious process. Learning about the Spirit is as simple — and as difficult — as coming to know ourselves.

Many spiritual mentors have preceded us and paved the way. Christ, Gandhi, Dag Hammarsjkold, Buddha, Ram Dass — and scores of other spiritual leaders have a burning interest in love and justice. They showed compassion in their lives and they inspired others by their trust and unwavering faith.

But all the sermons and stewardships and self-sacrifices become meaningless gestures and hollow noise if we do not have love and understanding for each other. This love has its origin in our primary relationships and pervades all our relationships.

How do we get in touch with the Spirit? The best way I know is through prayer. A time of prayer allows us to turn off the clatter in our minds so that we can integrate our experience with knowledge, and come to a more fundamental understanding of reality. Through prayer, we get back to basics. We accept the reality of life as a gift to be explored. Prayer eases the pressure and allows us to discern our priorities.

Prayer lets us see that God doesn't want us to DO something. He calls us to BE something. We must unfold and fulfill ourselves in all realms, in all aspects of our being. We must detect our specialness and nurture it.

In prayer we put aside our urge to rigidly control ourselves and others, and we respond to the Spirit. And when others pray and are touched by the Spirit, we learn from them, and they learn from us, for we have each known the truth of the Spirit.

Through prayer we come to know our power as persons, and accepting our power, we cease to be defensive and afraid. We can share power with others and not be diminished, impoverished or devitalized. Love grows between persons who come to know and accept their own power. The bond is one of mutual respect and caring, grounded in self-respect and self-care. Each of us has at least one other person who may never know love, except for our caring, our love. Just caring for that one person is a part of our mission.

Our power comes from within — it is not patched on from an outer source. Prayer allows us to become attuned to our inner strengths instead of looking for answers to life out there. As we look through prayer, we discover why we are special, and we see with greater clarity our special role in life. Life no longer perplexes us — we fit as snugly as a piece in a jigsaw puzzle.

As we come to know and accept ourselves, more and more of our inner spirit is released. This prayer, or releasing of our inner selves, it not reserved for specialists only — not only for ministers, saints, and mystics. Rather, it is a part inherent in each of us, awaiting discovery, like kindling awaiting the spark of awareness that will burst into a holy flame.

Our part in the meaning and mystery of life is to accept our essential powerlessness as controllers of creation, relationships, and destiny. Co-creators are Choicemakers, we accept the reality that we are part of life, and we flow with it.

We are energy cells, empowered to co-create, to work with a Creator to make meaning out of a world in need of change and redemption. It seems to be a law of spiritual life that our progress and direction come from a power within ourselves, and we can call that power God.

It seems to me that God lets us experience complete and total helplessness from time to time in order to remind us that as mortals we are powerless. But, at the same time, as persons using our emotional, physical and spiritual strengths, we are powerful. It is the source of freedom and faith, for freedom comes in accepting the reality of life, and the reality of powerlessness, not in controlling ourselves or others. And faith comes with our trust in the Spirit, that even though we are powerless, and our defenses crumble, our strength will prevail.

So often searchers miss this mystery of faith and meaning because they **cannot grasp it**. The irony is that we cannot grasp it — we can only **be grasped by it**. Faith is not an intellectual concept, something to understand, debate and collect data on. Faith is an attitude, a readiness, a willingness to accept unquestioningly. We sense it, feel it, and know it in ourselves and in others.

We feel faith . . .

> . . . When we are with someone we love;
> . . . When we are aware of the awesomeness of life, the thrill of rebirth (counselors sometimes see this);
> . . . When we get to the point of accepting ourselves.

Faith is the thread we hang onto when our life is falling apart. We experience it when we see the power of an ocean and the fragility of a dried-up dandelion. Faith is the warmth we feel when only one other person understands us and we know they accept us with open arms. We know the places and persons who bring about this feeling of being understood and accepted and loved. And we know that at such times we are in touch with the Spirit.

In describing this gift of faith, I am not saying that we **always** feel vibrant and confident. Even the most spiritual and most faithful among us at times have dark moments and gloomy moods. But with faith we have resilience, we have a reservoir of courage, strength and hope to draw on when we encounter pain. And we stand ready to be used by the Spirit in whatever plan God has for our lives.

When we feel the Spirit, it's like coming out of a fog. We know it can get foggy again, but we also know that there's sunshine behind the fog, and the mists will clear, and the Spirit will shine through once again. The light of the Spirit frees people, unburdens them, fosters growth and transformation, and allows them to become Choicemakers.

As spiritual beings and Choicemakers, we are all part of God's creation, God's plan. And we share an inner harmony and joy. But when we resist our spiritual side, when we falter at Choicemaking, we become more powerless. We are tense and restless and feel trapped in a morass — a spiritual void.

The Spirit comes to us like wind blowing through and through — taking away pretenses, games, phoniness. The Spirit leaves us raw, exposed, vulnerable and real. We are who we are. We are set free to figure out the meaning of life. And free people help set others free.

As spiritual Choicemakers, we have two tasks of the Spirit: The first is to carve out our own singular meaning in life, through growth and self-awareness. The second task is to open ourselves to the mystery of our place in redemption — the understanding of that brings the pain of a person's life to meaning and inner peace.

Dag Hammarsjkold wrote: *"The longest journey is the journey inward, for he who has chosen his destiny has started upon his quest for the source of his being."*

The journey is not grounded in belief. It is grounded in faith. Believers have a preconceived idea of how things should be. Those with faith, on the other hand, know only that life is rich and full of surprises. Believers cling to mottoes and creeds and officially-sanctioned truth. Those with faith are guided by a deep and abiding trust in the Higher Power and in their inner strength. Faith is a letting go and an acceptance of the life of the Spirit. It is a flowing with reality.

This life of the Spirit can be scary, for it involves venturing into unaccustomed realms. We feel tentative at first, a bit timorous, but in time we adjust. It is not easy to admit that our egos are limited, that there is a wider mainstream of existence that could touch us if we become the whole people we are meant to be. It's hard to drop our defenses and expose ourselves to a Spirit and to take risks, trusting to faith in the face of the unknown. And it's difficult to admit how much we need one another.

It is much easier and less risky to cling to familiar patterns and old conventional answers, even though new life is struggling to burst forth. The spirit of reality is already here, and so is new life.

If people were like notes of music, we could see that it takes a clear and specific note to produce a good sound, and when several notes come together, we have music. It takes persons becoming whole people to experience strength and beauty, and when these persons come together, we get a kind of harmony, a blending of balance and beauty. This is the music creation is all about. This is the chorus of Spirit we flow with, co-creators and Choicemakers in transformation. It's the only dance there is.

Transforming people remind me of springtime — in fact, I sometimes refer to them as Springtime People. No matter what the season is on the calendar, Springtime People radiate new life, new hope, new warmth and opportunity to others around them. Springtime People carry a biological clock that always reads: "Growth-Time: it's a good time to grow."

And Springtime People, transforming people, embody God's plan and purpose — that each of us should be free, free to become fully ourselves and to become a song of praise and celebration in every fiber of our being. When the sun shines on a garden, the flowers open to reveal marvels of intricate color and design. So it is with a transforming person, as he opens in the warm glow of the Spirit to love of self and others.

No more inner emptiness and aimlessness. No more spiritual void. From a transforming heart there comes a unique melody, a song of harmony and self-containment welling up and flowing from inner tranquility. That harmony, that music — that's the joy that crowns Creation.

Sin is whatever holds you back from your
potential.

Sorrows are stepping-stones for greater
things.

People feel unimportant and frustrated
because they have given *their power away,
not because someone* took it. . .

11

Happiness, Wholeness, Holiness

Happiness, wholeness and holiness are all related, all intertwined in meaning . . .

We are happiness questers. Our mad and impassioned pursuit of happiness leads us up blind alleys and cul-de-sacs. The harder we search, the more frantic our efforts become, the more happiness seems to elude us. While we seek for happiness Out There, it comes to us on tiptoe in quiet moments of repose and catches us all unaware.

Definitions do not help much when talking about happiness. I prefer to think about some of the little things — and not so little things — that make me happy:

   . . . Receiving a hug

   . . . Petting a warm puppy

   . . . Landing at the airport (what a relief!)

   . . . Hearing the voices of my children on the phone

   . . . Hearing my husband come home from work

   . . . Visiting with my mother

   . . . Walking at sunset

   . . . Falling asleep after a long day

   . . . Being trusted by my clients

. . . Getting a letter from a friend
. . . Listening to music.

As you can see, happiness comes in great variety. There's nothing mysterious about it. It may arise from the most ordinary, everyday circumstances. Happiness can be brief, or it can last a whole day. Let's explore now some of the qualities of happiness.

Happiness is filled with paradox. To get it, we must forget trying to grab at it directly. It seems to always come as a by-product. It comes when we get absorbed in something worthwhile outside ourselves. It comes when we get in touch with our inner self, when we are touched by intimacy.

Happiness is not necessarily associated with pleasure. We all know of the grumpy, angry, chronically dissatisfied millionaires and jet-setters who have much money. They have tasted every pleasure, they have pursued sensation to the limit, and yet they sometimes continue to be bored, frustrated and fundamentally unhappy. To have material wealth or not have material wealth is irrelevant to spiritual wealth.

Happiness does not come from being a passive person, one who escapes reality through alcohol or drugs, money or power. Passivity and withdrawal bring pain and violence, rather than peace and contentment. The happy person must be actively engaged with life, despite all its difficulties.

Holiness is bound up with struggle. It flows from a life of purpose. That is why there is a special contentment in the lives of people who strive to love each other. Even when they have debts, illness, disappointment, and monotony, they are happy knowing that they have dedicated their energies to a worthy commitment. The individual who strives only to save his own life, to grab hold of happiness without letting go of himself, is the one happiness passes by.

Happiness is not made for one class of people, for those of a certain race, or color, or creed. Neither is it the crowning reward for a perfect person, or for someone especially deserving. Even with great limitations, one can attain happiness once the person recognizes his weakness, whether physical, spiritual, or emotional. Once it is admitted and faced with courage, one can be on the way to peace and holiness.

There are many people who have had to make their way back in a recovery program. They faced their reality and found a new wholeness — a new holiness — in the process.

Happiness, holiness and wholeness are not reserved for the perfect person and the ideal condition. Rather, holiness comes when one's self and one's life situation is faced honestly and realistically. Holiness is being willing to experience each day in trust and faith in a Higher Power. It means being fully aware of who we are, and making whatever choices we have to make in order to live a full and satisfying life.

Wholeness means using our choicemaking skills to address the major areas of our life. Wholeness comes from paying attention to each of our self-worth potentials.

Whole Person Wheel:
Personal Aspects of Self-Worth

On the following page is a diagram of the whole person. It is a diagram made up of disconnected lines. No matter how the human person is divided for the sake of clearer understanding, there is a need to note that everything affects everything else. The difficulty with a drawing is that it is static. The system of powers within a person is very much in motion, a dynamic that's creative and capable of almost anything.

Congruent communication, honest, open communication, is a necessity for a healthy person. It has an interesting by-product. The by-product of congruence with others is a step into the search for meaning within oneself. A person is not only a member of a system which includes other people. He is also a system within himself. He is a system of energies or powers. Each power acts and interacts with all the others. The harmony sought after within a person is called wholeness.

Each personal power has its own importance. Each exists along with the others, and not at their expense. Each can give richness to the others. The powers within a person are the following:

The Mental Power: The ability to remember the past, to have ideas in the present, and to plan, to imagine, and to dream in the future.

The Will Power: The ability to choose to do or not to do, to decide and not to decide, to follow through or change direction, to place values.

The Emotional Power: The ability to allow oneself to feel the highs and the lows, the joys and the sorrows, the love and hate, the cautions and vulnerabilities of life.

The Physical Power: The ability to move, to be active sexually, to build surroundings, to feed oneself, to live in time and space.

The Social Power: The ability to develop and maintain close relationships, to love and be loved.

The Spiritual Power: The ability to search for the meaning of life, the meaning of the "I" that a Higher Power gives me. The Spiritual Power is the channel to a meaning greater than myself.

Enlightenment is the reward given to those who seek meaning. These persons have a two-fold existence. They conscientiously perform their work in the world. And they are inwardly immersed in spiritual peace.

In *The Shoes of the Fisherman*, Morris West spelled out what it means to be enlightened:

> *It costs so much to be a full human being that there are very few who have the enlightenment, or the courage, to pay the price . . . One has to abandon altogether the search for security, and reach out to the risk of living with both arms. One has to embrace the world like a lover, and yet demand no easy return of love. One has to accept pain as a condition of existence. One has to court doubt and darkness as the cost of knowing. One needs a will stubborn in conflict, but apt always to total acceptance of every consequence of living and dying.*

We are all artists and Choicemakers when it comes to designing our growth in freedom. Love, freedom, risk and choice — it's easy to talk about them, easy to use the words. But hard to put into practice. We are tempted to let success, money, prestige, power, old hurts, current comfort and security consume our time and energy, and keep us from following our vision of freedom and spiritual awakening.

Spirituality is Whatever You Take to be Your Ultimate Concern.

Your spiritual attitude is found at the point of conviction where you define the values in your experience that are worth living and risking for. Authentic personal freedom opens the door to true spirituality. And, in spirituality, the Choicemaker finds Freedom.

A Choicemaker does not measure freedom by particular choices or risks, but instead the Choicemaker finds freedom in the sheer intensity of the moment when the person, when the Choicemaker, transformed and transforming, breaks through to a new level of awareness and consciousness.

And it only happens . . .

One Choice at a Time

One Change at a Time

and

One Day at a Time

Epilogue

The soul is restless and will keep us restless until we are fulfilled.

*I had absolutely nothing to
back me up except a
deeply rooted resolution and
belief. My belief was formed
by life and by my experience
and a deep feeling within me.*

*I listened to my inner self,
my God and many others and
did what I had to do . . .
and it was good for me . . .
and good for others.*

— Sharon

NOTES
Prologue — A Personal Word

Page iii: *Another Chance*, published by Science and Behavior Books, P.O. Box 11457, Palo Alto, CA 94306.

Page iv: "Anthony Padavano . . .", theologian and professor at Immaculate Conception Seminary, Darlington, New Jersey. Author of *Dawn Without Darkness*, Paulist Press, 1971, and *Belief in Human Life*, Paulist Press.

Page viii: "Sam Hardy . . .," co-director of Turn-Off, a drug rehabilitation ranch, Desert Hot Springs, California. Sam's comment came at one of my workshops.

Chapter One: Varieties of Co-Dependency

Page 10: "A *Dictionary of Words about Alcohol* . . .," Second edition, by Mark Keller, Mairi McCormick and Vera Efron. Rutgers Center of Alcohol Studies, New Brunswick, NJ (1982). The *Dictionary* does include a sort entry on **family therapy** — about half as long as the entry on **koumiss** ("A nutritious fermented drink said by Herodotus to be known to the Scythians, made from mare's or camel's milk and drunk widely by Asiatic nomadic tribes.")

Page 11: "Sondra Smalley . . .," Director of the Dependencies Institute of Minnesota and consultant for the Program in Human Sexuality at the University of Minnesota Medical School. Paraphrase from her lecture to International Doctors in A.A., Minneapolis, MN, August, 1984.

"Robert Subby . . .," Director, Family Systems Center, Minneapolis, MN. Quote from *Focus on Family*, November/December/1983.

Page 30: "Cannon . . . Selye . . .," see especially Walter Cannon's pioneering book, *The Wisdom of the Body*, 1932, and Hans Selye's writings on stress, particularly *The Stress of Life*, 1956. Because of the ubiquity of stress-related disorders, stress-reduction has become a major industry in the fields of health care and disease prevention.

"Dr. Charles Whitfield . . .," see his articles, "Co-Dependency: An Emerging Illness Among Professionals," in *Focus on Alcohol and Drug Issues*, May/June, 1983, and "The Patient with Alcoholism and Other Drug Problems," Year Book Medical Publishers, Chicago, 1982.

Page 33: "Intervention . . .," see my book, *Another Chance*, for a detailed account of intervention with a Dependent (especially pages 150-162).

Page 39: "Dry drunk syndrome" . . . Terence Gorski sees the dry drunk as an integral part of the "Relapse Syndrome." For the role of nutrition in the dry drunk syndrome, see "The Dry Drunk Syndrome: A Toximolecular Interpretation," Mark Worden and Gayle Rosellini, *The Journal of Orthomolecular Psychiatry*, 9(1):41-47, 1980.

Chapter Two: Young Children of Alcoholics

Page 49: "All Children Learn . . ." — Children born into alcoholic families may also be affected by the

Fetal Alcohol Syndrome. The U.S. Surgeon General has issued an advisory, cautioning pregnant women to abstain from alcohol during the course of pregnancy. The National Council on Alcoholism, the National Institute on Alcohol Abuse and Alcoholism, and the American Medical Association, along with numerous other groups have issued similar warnings. According to University of Washington research scientist Ruth Little, no safe level of alcohol has been established for pregnant women.

In addition, children born into an alcoholic home may have an heredity predisposition for alcoholism. Research by Donald Goodwin, M.D., and Marc Schuckit, M.D., has shown that children of alcoholics are particularly susceptible to alcoholism — and that this susceptibility is hereditary.

Page 53: "Timmen Cermak . . .," San Francisco psychiatrist and first president of the National Association of Children of Alcoholics.

Page 54: "Tarpley Richards . . .," a social worker with Counseling Associates, Inc., Washington, D.C., quoted in a Washington Post feature story June 6, 1985.

Page 67: "Claudia Black . . .," one of the early leaders in the children of alcoholics movement. Dr. Black is author of *My Dad Loves Me, My Dad Has A Disease* and *It Will Never Happen To Me*. She is also a founding board member of the National Association of Children of Alcoholics.

Chapter Four: Adult Children of Alcoholics

Page 113: "Dr. Harry Tiebout . . .," see "Ego Factors in Surrender to Alcoholism," *Quarterly Journal of Studies on Alcoholism*, 15, pp. 610-621, 1954.

Page 115: "Janet Woititz . . .," see her book, *Adult Children of Alcoholics*, published by Health Communications, Inc., 1721 Blount Road, Suite 1, Pompano Beach, FL 33069.

Page 122: "Bob Subby . . ." — Bob wrote this after an adult child he knew closely had committed suicide.

Page 125: "Ben Whitney . . .," a law student and participant in one of my Reconstruction programs, July 1984.

Chapter Six: Family Therapy and Individual Recovery

Page 137: ". . . Role of family members . . ." See *The Biology of Alcoholism*, edited by Benjamin Kissin and Henri Begleiter, Volumes 4 and 5: *Social Aspects of Alcoholism* and *The Treatment and Rehabilitation of the Chronic Alcoholic*, Plenum Press, 1976, 1978.

Page 138: "Margaret Cork . . ." Her book, *The Forgotten Children*, was published by the Addiction Research Foundation, Toronto, Canada. Cork makes a point often overlooked by alcoholism professionals: A parent's recovery does not automatically insure that the child's lot improves, or that family life gets better.

Page 141: "Women alcoholics . . ." See *The Invisible Alcoholics* by Marian Sandmaier, McGraw-Hill, 1980; *A Dangerous Pleasure* by Geraldine Youcha, Hawthorne Books, 1975; and *Alcohol and Drug Problems in Women*, Vol. 5, *Research Advances in Alcohol and Drug Problems*, edited by Oriana Josseau Kalant, Plenum Books, 1980.

Page 169: "James Michener . . .," *The Fires of Spring*, Random House, 1962.

Page 180: "Anthony Padavano . . .," see note, page 4.

Chapter Seven: Ongoing Recovery

Page 197: "Dr. M. Scott Peck . . .," medical director of New Milford Hospital Mental Health Clinic and psychiatrist in private practice, New Milford, CT. Quote from his book, *The Road Less Traveled*, Simon and Schuster, 1978.

Page 201: "Serendipity . . .," being disposed to making happy and unexpected discoveries by accident. "Serendipity" was coined by 19th-Century British author, Horace Walpole, who noted that the princes in an old fairy tale, "The Three Princes of Serendip," were "always making discoveries of things they were not in quest of."

Chapter Eight: Barriers to Recovery

Page 209: "Lewis Carroll . . .," see *Through the Looking Glass* by Lewis Carroll, in *The Complete Works of Lewis Carroll*, Vintage Books (1976), p. 166.

Chapter Eleven: Happiness, Wholeness, Holiness

Page 246: "Morris West . . .," see *The Shoes of the Fisherman* by Morris L. West, Dell Publishing Co. (1963), p. 195-196.